KINGDOM
OF THE
ICE BEAR

KINGDOM
—OF THE—
ICE BEAR

A PORTRAIT OF THE ARCTIC
Hugh Miles and Mike Salisbury

UNIVERSITY OF TEXAS PRESS, AUSTIN

By arrangement with the
BRITISH BROADCASTING CORPORATION

To Sue, Vyv and our children,
who had to put up with our absence
for so many months

International Standard Book Number 0-292-70393-7
Copyright © 1985 by Hugh Miles and Mike Salisbury

First University of Texas Press Edition, 1986

Requests for permission to reproduce material from
this work should be sent to
Permissions, University of Texas Press,
Box 7819, Austin, Texas 78713-7819

Set in 11/13pt Linotron Sabon
by Ace Filmsetting Limited, Frome and printed
in England by Chorley and Pickersgill Limited, Leeds.

CONTENTS

OUR SPECIAL THANKS

This book recounts the story of two years' filming to make a series of three programmes for television on the Arctic environment and its wonderful wildlife. Any film project relies almost entirely on teamwork, and never more so than in the Arctic. The extreme climate and remote locations ensure that the experiences are shared, and also encourages those apparently primitive human virtues of humbleness, sensitivity, comradeship and kindness. Mike and I were given so much help and friendship that we didn't just survive the hardships, we thoroughly enjoyed them, and that is in large part due to the generous attitude of so many good people. Our list is inevitably long, but no less sincere for that.

We must give special thanks to Ian Stirling for having encouraged our venture from the start and seen it through to the end. He gave freely of his valuable time, knowledge and experience, as did those other fine Arctic scientists Thor Larsen, Stewart MacDonald, Frank Miller, Anne Gunn, Buster Welch, Norman Negus, Pat Berger, Andy Rode, Christian Vibe and Glen Cota.

We received much practical help, without which our project would never have got off the ground. Firstly, there is George Hobson of the Polar Continental Shelf Project and his staff at Resolute, especially Barry Hough. Salmita and Lupin Mines provided us with warm homes and a welcome, Åge Christensen of the Danish Government ensured that our Greenland expedition was a success, Gier Paulsen worked hard to make sure our skidoos kept going in Svalbard, and Harald Ottensen kept us in touch on the radio. Bezal and Terry Jesudasen did much for us when we were based in Resolute, and Terry Woolf when in Yellowknife.

Many officials and organisations gave us their blessing, notably the Norwegian Governor of Svalbard, who showed sympathy and understanding for our problems. We received much advice from numerous scientists in the Canadian Wildlife Service, and members of the Government of the Northwest Territories were equally generous with their help and knowledge. The Arctic Petroleum Operators' Association co-ordinated our research into oil development, and Air Canada and Pacific Western Airlines were most generous in handling mountains of excess baggage.

Flying in the Arctic is nearly always fraught with difficulties, and to the many pilots who flew us safely through the hazards a special thank you, particularly to the pilots of Polar Shelf, Aero Arctic and Latham Island Airways.

Our films would never have been made without the BBC's support and Peter Jones' encouragement, but Mike and I are particularly indebted to Judy Copeland, who for three years ensured that we were in the right place at the right time and, when we returned, provided us with thoroughly efficient and enthusiastic assistance. Judy and Margaret Clarke had the unenviable task of typing the manuscript for this book, and Hilary Duguid the even worse task of trying to make sense of the words; thank you to them all for making a potential ordeal a pleasure.

As for the films, we received some lovely sequences from several photographers around the world, with especially valuable contributions from Martin Saunders, Michael Richards and Owen Newman. We spent many creative weeks with our film editors, Martin Elsbury and his assistant Ian Butcher, and we are grateful that they made this complex task so enjoyable. Terry Oldfield composed the music with great sensitivity, Peter Copeland skilfully mixed together the sound tracks and Paul Johnson created the excellent title sequence and other graphics.

Grateful as we are to all the above, we hold a special affection for those who have shared our experiences in the field, for without their good humour, patience and kindness, wildlife film-making would have become a dour struggle. We remember the caribou searches with Doug Heard, Frank Miller, Anne Gunn and Eric Broughton. Polar bears provided many moments of agony and ecstasy, shared firstly with Rasmus Hansson and Birger Amundsen in Svalbard, then in Canada with Andy Derocher and Steve Miller at Churchill and with Ian Stirling, Dennis Andriashek, Wendy Calvert and Cheryl Spencer at Radstock Bay.

Greenland experiences were shared with Mike Read and David Cabot's expedition, and we had many happy moments out on the ice at Resolute. The Fisheries & Oceans team there consisted of Buster and Cathy Welch, Martin Bergmann, Aziz Kheraj, John Jorgenson, Lynda Scharf, Trish Lewis, Dan Pike, Martin Curtis and the late Sam Idlout, all of whom helped greatly with the filming. At Arctic Bay the filming was made both safe and entertaining by Glen Williams and Jonah Oyukuluk, while another Inuk, George Qulant, gave invaluable assistance at Igloolik. It is perhaps appropriate that the Timothy Idlout family should be the last we name, for they live out on the land throughout the year.

We hope that those we haven't mentioned in person will not think that this implies a lack of gratitude. They too are part of the memorable experiences we have tried to share, and if a book is a way of saying thank you, we hope it will prove enjoyable and that those many kind people who helped us will feel the films do justice to their contribution.

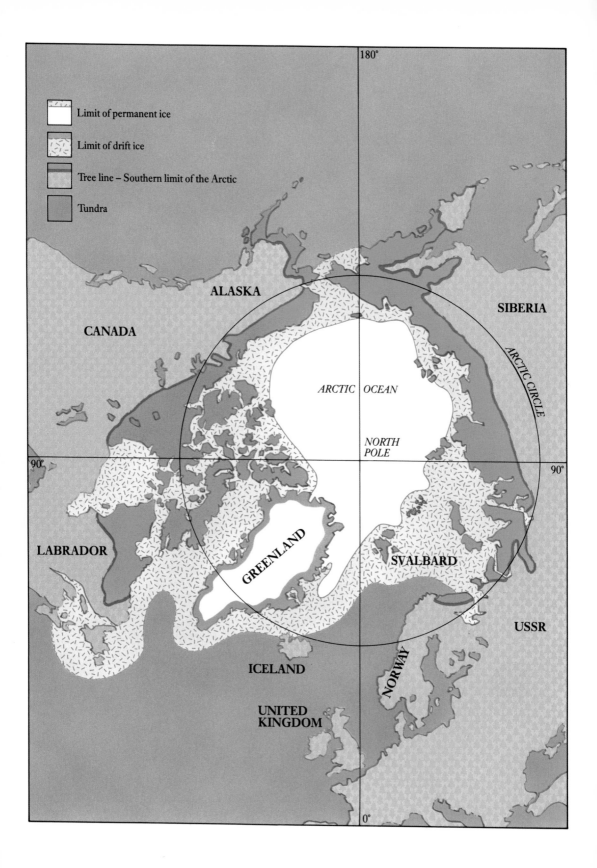

TO THE LAND OF BEYOND

'Mike and I are alone, surrounded by a frozen world in which humans become totally insignificant. The awesome expanse of landscape and sky merge into blankness, the complete horizon lost in a white infinity; from this spot there is nothing but ice and snow, all the way to the North Pole.

'We take off again and fly over a world which is entombed in winter frost – land and lake look alike – it is uncompromisingly cold. These are the Canadian Barren Grounds, once described as the Earth's most uncivilised land, an almost limitless expanse of treeless tundra, ten times the size of England. The Barrens sprawl across the North American continent from Alaska to Labrador, an immense, undulating plain – a land without people. Even at the start of this century, less was known of this place than the remotest districts of darkest Africa. Searching for caribou in this featureless waste seems hopeless.

'We have already flown north-east from Yellowknife for two hours, passing over the vast spruce forests in which the caribou are supposed to spend the winter. Now we are in the area where conditions are too severe for trees to grow, but have seen no sign of life. We feel distinctly daunted, although on paper the task appeared simple. The schedule reads: 24–29 March – film caribou leaving tree-line, and hopefully wolves. We had expected problems with the wolves, but not the caribou.

'After yet another hour's flying we have seen only the occasional caribou track, but of the vast congregations there is no sign. We cover a wide area of 200 square kilometres and see nothing – failure stares us in the face, and this is only day one.

'We fly in a wide arc and return south-west to the edge of the trees, where 100-year-old spruces barely reach the height of a man. This is the "land of the little sticks", where white monotony is fractured by splinters of tree and rock. Then, as if they have always been there, we discover thirty-six caribou walking across the frozen surface of Drybones Lake and circle to find a smooth place to land. On final approach it becomes clear that the wind has raised snow into one-metre ridges and the frost has hardened them like concrete. We bounce and slither alarmingly – it is more of a crash than a landing, but we come to an uncertain stop with body and machine still intact.

'Stepping out into the icy breeze, the air crackles in our nostrils, breath freezes in our beards, our faces become frostbitten. Gloved hands grow rapidly chill when in contact with metal equipment, lenses and camera start to seize, and it is only −26°C. Next week we head 1500 kilometres north, where it will be −46°C. We hope we will survive this ordeal.

'Though it is the spring migration of the caribou that we have come to film, there is nothing spring-like in the air apart from the weak sunshine. But hostile though the Barrens are to us, to the animals that live there it is home. Creatures like the caribou have adapted through centuries of thaw and freeze to survive, even to flourish, in comparative comfort. These deer of the north have one of the finest insulating coats of any animal, the hairs dense and hollow in order to reduce the loss of heat; they even have hair on their ears and nose. They lay on fat reserves in the autumn, which also act as insulation and should last them until rich feeding returns next summer. Their feet are large, and their hoof can split and act as a snow shoe and, being sharp-edged, also gives them a good grip on icy slopes.

'Caribou certainly wander on snow-covered frozen lakes with ease, but for me it is unreliable – supporting the weight of myself and camera, but occasionally letting me down into knee-deep powder. The animals appear indifferent to my floundering presence a kilometre away, but I decide to approach with caution, stalking them through the trees. The snow here is waist deep, so I don snow shoes and creep closer. Now, far from indifferent, the caribou raise heads and tails in alert posture and unhurriedly filter away across the frozen lake, well out of camera range. Their ghost-like, pale fawn melts into the gathering haze. It is not an auspicious start to our ambitious project, and with the light fading, we have to return to Yellowknife. We do so in sober reflection on our failure, wondering just what we have taken on.'

So reads our diary for 24 March 1983. It was day one of a six-week expedition to the far north, and the first of sixteen such expeditions Mike and I were to make over the two years that it took to complete filming. We remember that first day with affection, for it marked the beginning of an obsession with the Arctic from which we might never really escape. That silent world of subtle beauty has captured men's imaginations throughout history, and it was a poet, Robert Service, who called it 'The Land of Beyond'.

> Thank God! there is always a Land of Beyond,
> For us who are true to the trail,
> A vision to seek, a beckoning peak,
> A farness that never will fail . . .

Robert Service was a bank clerk from the Yukon, Mike and I are wildlife film-makers from England, intent on trying to illustrate something of the magic of the Arctic. But that first day, in awe of the sheer enormity of the place, and the intense discomfort, we began to understand why no television company in the world had ever really attempted to make a comprehensive series on Arctic wildlife. Until that first day the omission seemed extraordinary – the last great wilderness still largely unexploited, an area in which huge herds of wild animals still roam free, and whales and seals swim undisturbed. There are no man-made boundaries, the area is enormous, and still largely unspoiled.

Our plan was to make three one-hour films for BBC Television on this wildlife, and what follows is the story of how we went about it. It is based on the diaries Mike and I wrote during two years' filming, but we have condensed the events into one calendar year to give a better impression of the seasonal progression and to show how the animals and birds live and flourish in that harsh but wonderful land.

The first of the films was to be based on the marine ecosystem, the second film would concentrate on the ecology of the Arctic land mass, and the third on man's relationship with the wildlife and the environment, both historically and in the present day.

The 'star' of the first film would naturally be the polar bear, for it stands at the top of the marine food chain. Polar bears eat seals, which eat fish, which eat plankton, which 'blooms' when the sun shines on the ice. Above all, the polar bear is a magnificent beast, the largest carnivore in the world and a symbol of the Arctic since the last great ice age relinquished a partial hold on this land of ice and snow.

The southern limit of the Arctic is the area where weather conditions allow trees to grow and the resulting 'tree-line' circles the globe, winding through Alaska, Canada, Scandinavia and Russia. This was our boundary for the second film and the caribou would make a natural 'star', for its migration would take our story through the seasons and our centre of interest from the trees in the south to the 'High Arctic' in the far north. It is here that the summer sun brings a dramatic transformation to the land, and where, during this brief season, all life must raise its young and plants flower and set seed before the long nights of a nine-month winter return.

The caribou would also figure prominently in the third film, for the survival of many native peoples once depended on their appearance during the annual migration. If the caribou failed to materialise, the Eskimos – or Inuit as they now prefer to be called – would starve. The caribou are still an important part of their culture and a vital link with the past.

Mike and I were keen to do more than just make two 'pretty' films about the Arctic, so we devised this third film in order to look at some of the issues of the day. Has the influence of western culture changed the Inuit's relationship with the animals? Can Arctic animals such as caribou and polar bears be successfully 'managed'? Can the abundant mineral riches be extracted without despoiling and polluting the Arctic lands and seas? There are so many conflicting interests in the Arctic today that we considered this the most challenging programme of the three.

11

*The Barrens
in winter*

*Far right: the
sun returns*

12

With the basic concept decided upon, we read extensively about Arctic wildlife and ecology before producing three 'treatments'. These were sent to some of the most experienced scientists in the Arctic and their advice was to be particularly valuable. Their names read like a roll of honour. There was Christian Vibe for Greenland, Thor Larsen for Svalbard, Stewart MacDonald and Ian Stirling for Canada, and, to our delight, they all agreed to be our scientific advisers. There were many others who were to help us during the project, but more of them as the story unfolds.

In January 1983 we did a quick tour round to visit our advisers and discuss the treatments, and many valuable ideas and corrections came out of the meetings. They agreed that our 'biological concepts' were correct, but their unanimous impression that our intentions were also ambitious seemed to be expressed in tones more cautionary than we would have liked. We comforted ourselves with the thought that if we didn't aim high we would not be honouring the ambitions of the BBC. Above all, even if reducing something as magnificent as the Arctic down to just three hours of television was bound to seem superficial, even trivial, we felt we must try to do justice to those who were to give us so much help.

There were various ways of tackling the project regarding manpower, either in the modern way by injecting considerable production control and using numerous cameramen for the different sequences and countries, or by using just a small team. As Mike and I were anticipating enjoying ourselves on the various expeditions, we decided to be selfish and do as much as possible of the filming ourselves, only resorting to other cameramen in the second year – notably Martin Saunders – when it was necessary to be in two places at once. We were all 'held together' back at base by Judy Copeland, so for most of the three years there were just Mike, Judy and myself, a very small team for such a large project. But perhaps the films would have a coherence of style which might be lacking with any other method.

Any film is part art and part science, a combination of knowledge, planning, logistics, anticipation, patience, persistence, hard work and luck. But in the Arctic there is also the intense cold, and the technical and physical problems that this could bring. The camera and lenses were easily 'winterised' with lightweight lubricants and we even had an environmental housing developed which would protect the camera from snow, and also provide heating. Batteries are always a problem in the cold, so we had additional cells put in each, and insulated pouches made to keep out the chill.

Film equipment taken care of, we now had the more difficult challenge of our own physical preparation. It is not that we were exactly unfit, but the wrong side of forty. We were not quite tall, muscular and 'macho', but rather a shade short, fat and hairy! Perhaps the Glenmore Lodge Outward Bound School in Scotland could knock us into shape. So off we set for a week's survival course on top of the Cairngorms – the nearest to Arctic conditions we could afford.

The brochure frightened us by stressing how fit we had to be, so we both made a half-hearted attempt at training before heading north. This only seemed to make our bodies even more reluctant to climb mountains, and it was Bob Barton's misfortune to be allocated the job of trying to ensure that we survived the survival course. Our schedule for the week included the use of ice axe and crampons, map reading, cross-country skiing, snow shelters, igloo building, rope work, river crossings, climbing and various other alarming techniques which my mind prefers not to remember.

The first day found us on a steep icy slope, sliding down in various postures, the most exciting of which was head down on our backs – as the momentum increased, the urgent necessity to be able to use an ice axe as a break soon ensured that we would include this as essential equipment on our expeditions. Our proficiency improved rapidly, mainly to avoid climbing all the way back up the mountain. When we did have to climb up, crampons had the most amazing properties of adhesion, even on almost vertical ice, and on more gentle slopes, cutting steps with an ice axe was a skill that was to prove useful both in Canada and Svalbard.

We were also anticipating having to ski in Svalbard, so Bob struggled to teach us the rudiments. Both Mike and I loved downhill skiing, but trying to control cross-country skis on an icy piste proved entertaining. One day we decided to try out our white, windproof camouflage jackets, and some by-standers, apparently impressed by Mike's technique and appearance, said, 'Oh, look – Arctic Patrol,' whereupon Mike fell in a heap and had to be extricated from a tangle of skis and sticks. We used 'skins' to climb to the summit of Cairngorm on skis, then bombed down the other side on virgin powder snow, a pleasure that was tempered by the knowledge that every foot down was one that would have to be climbed back up.

Bob chose a day of complete 'white-out' to test our map reading, no doubt so we couldn't cheat. We staggered around on the plateau using 'time', 'compass' and 'counting our paces' in order to ensure we did not step off the edge of the mountain. It was cold, wet, and windy, fairly Arctic really, and to complete the illusion we learnt to build snow shelters and picnicked in a previously built overnight snow house. The icy roof dripped, and we shivered wearily; we did not relish the thought of having to survive in such an emergency shelter in the Arctic!

Clothing was going to be of vital importance if we were not only to survive the cold, but work in it too. Bob gave us lots of valuable advice, for he is an experienced expedition climber and mountaineer, but we also spent a day with the Royal Marine Commandos in Plymouth. Their regular Arctic patrols in Norway had made them the leaders regarding survival in cold climates, and they passed on their extensive knowledge with great generosity.

One thing that they did stress was the need to carry a survival kit every time we ventured far from base camp or undertook any journey, be it on skis, skidoo, helicopter or plane. A tragedy in Norway only the previous week, when three members of an army patrol died because they failed to heed this advice, stressed the importance of survival equipment and made us quite certain that cold can kill. We have compiled the following list for those who might also be venturing north:

1   Candle for freezing interior of snow-hole and for light and warmth.
    Make sure that there is ventilation.
2   Waterproof matches.
3   Survival bag – either polythene or spaceblanket material.
4   Small torch.
5   48-hour emergency high protein rations × 2.
6   1 sleeping bag each.
7   1 outer waterproof cover or Gortex tunnel tent.
8   1 sleeping mat, 30mm thickness.
9   1 tent cover.
10 1 length of nylon cord.
11 1 flask with hot soup or similar in insulated flask carrier.
12 1 small portable cooker filled with fuel.
13 1 small polythene container extra fuel.
14 2 or 3 emergency light sticks.
15 Compass.

    Plus essential personal gear:
16 Snow goggles.
17 Headcover.
18 Whistle.
19 Heavy knife, for cutting snow holes, banging in tent pegs, cutting off
    frostbitten fingers! etc.

All that fits into a rucksack and despite the fact that we already had
sufficient to carry with the film equipment, we always had that gear with us
(well, almost always). So, armed with the survival gear, and woollen under-
wear, numerous thin but warm layers, down-filled sleeping bags and trousers,
thick parkas, special insulated boots called 'mukluks', snow shoes, snow saws,
climbing rope, ice axes, etc., all that remained was to have a quick practice on a
range with Magnum .44 pistols and .308 rifles and we reckoned we were ready
for anything. So prepared, we set off with mountains of equipment and some
apprehension, with the parting words from my wife Sue that we were just a
'couple of old has-beens' ringing in our ears.

24 March 1983 found us floundering in the snow of the Canadian Barrens,
becoming rapidly aware of the problems of filming in the Arctic. Despite the
disappointment of a failure on that first day, we were not really surprised, for
we had been warned by our guide, Doug Heard of the Northwest Territories'
Wildlife Service, that we might never find the caribou. Many others, including
himself, had failed in the past and, though it might seem impossible to lose
130,000 caribou, the land is just awesomely vast. However, Mike and I
reflected that our first experience was very much the essence of the Arctic, and
we would try to illustrate this sense of infinite space in our films.
    Armed with such positive thoughts, 25 March found us once again
searching over the trees, but without success. Fearing the caribou had already
headed out into the Barrens, we searched beyond the tree-line and found more

Caribou leave the trees

Below left: the trails head north

Below: the two 'has beens' and their 'gear'

17

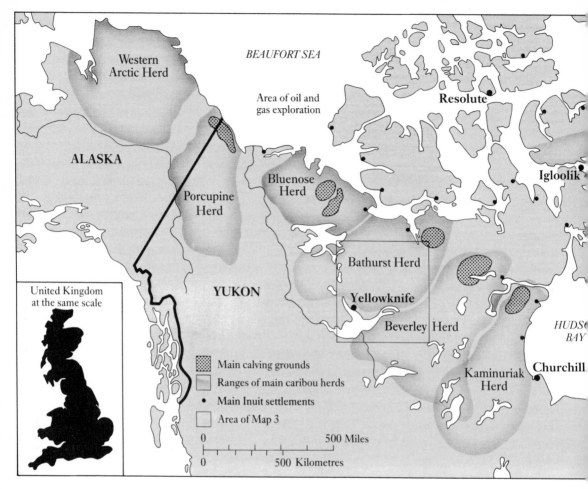

Western Arctic Herd

BEAUFORT SEA

Resolute

Area of oil and gas exploration

ALASKA

Porcupine Herd

Bluenose Herd

Igloolik

United Kingdom at the same scale

YUKON

Bathurst Herd

Yellowknife

Beverley Herd

HUDSON BAY

Main calving grounds

Ranges of main caribou herds

• Main Inuit settlements

Area of Map 3

Churchill

Kaminuriak Herd

0   500 Miles

0   500 Kilometres

than a thousand animals some 100 kilometres to the north. Doug had never recorded such an early departure before, and we cursed silently; but why a record year this year? Perhaps the deep snow in the trees had forced them out, for food is easier to reach in the Barrens, where storms sweep ridges clear of snow. We could not land anywhere near the animals due to the rocky terrain, so we returned to Yellowknife and resorted to Plan B.

There are seven major herds of caribou in the north of Canada and Alaska, two of which are within reasonable striking distance of Yellowknife. So having failed with the Bathurst Herd, we hoped the Beverley Herd, some way to the East, might still be in the trees and give us the sequence we needed.

We had previously made contact with Frank Miller and Anne Gunn, two very fine Arctic biologists who worked for the Canadian Wildlife Service and Northwest Territories' Wildlife Service respectively. They often joined forces to work with caribou, and were at that time counting the Beverley Herd near Porter Lake. Rather foolishly, they had offered to help us if we came unstuck with the Bathurst Herd. So, unannounced for the radios were not functioning, the next day saw us slithering to a halt on the ice outside their log cabin. Their

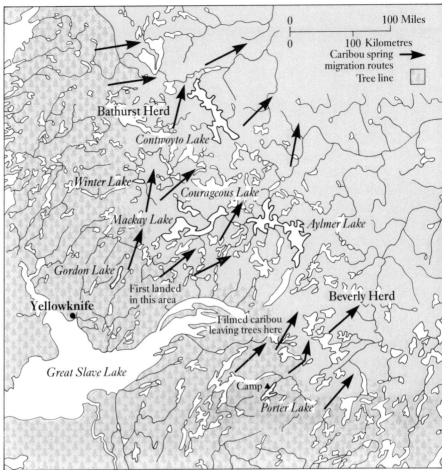

surprise (they hid their horror well) as the little plane disgorged Mike and me and the usual mountain of gear was not unexpected. But, not for the last time, we were made immensely grateful for the hospitality and help we received from busy Canadian scientists.

Within minutes they had completely reorganised their work schedule to enable us to use their helicopter. Fortunately the herds were still in the trees in good numbers, and there were even wolves with them. With hopes high, we flew north and, seeing four wolves near an old Inuit hunting camp on No Name Lake, we landed and tried to film them. Though less fearful than I had anticipated, they still disappeared with remarkable speed. Frank dropped us by some herds of caribou and we were just stalking into position to be close to their migration route when a snow squall threatened and we had to be rescued. We were disappointed, for it was our first chance of a close encounter with the caribou.

Next day we found a group of over 3000 caribou out in the Barrens, about 100 kilometres north of our camp, and landed the helicopter out of sight behind a ridge. The temperature was close to −30°C, the snow the consistency of concrete, but the caribou tramped slowly northward, stopping

19

when their lowered noses smelt food, and chipping through the snow and ice with their front hooves to reach it. They eat lichens, and stay alive on this dry, tasteless pale yellow plant – tasteless at least to us, for I tried it and found it distinctly unpalatable. But they search for it constantly and in this way move slowly north, travelling about 15 kilometres a day. This constant movement also serves to preserve the delicate lichens from over-grazing.

Though the urge to reach the calving grounds is with them, they cannot afford to hurry, for they are lean and hungry after the winter and have little spare fuel to burn. Their destination is some 600 kilometres to the north-east and there will be hardships to face before they reach it in early June. Soft snow might hamper their progress, blizzards will halt them completely; there is little food in that spare land and the wolves will be ever present.

Wolves rely entirely on caribou meat to survive the winter. They follow the herds relentlessly, watching for lame, sick or weary animals and then running the unfortunate down as a pack, either in a relay system, or by driving it into an ambush. Those caribou that reach the calving grounds are the strong ones. We saw only four wolves, perhaps the same ones as on the previous day, but Frank and Anne saw thirty the day after we left – such is the luck of film-making.

We returned to the tree-line and found many other herds also flowing north; the exodus was on, the renewal of life ensured for one more year. We filmed the sequence we needed from the top of a snow-covered hill, watching the long lines filter out from the trees, each following the footsteps of the previous occupant, for in this way they save energy.

Some describe the sedate walk of the caribou as a plod, and they do look somewhat dejected as they search, head down, for food. Only when threatened by wolves, or by our over-enthusiastic approach, do they look up, and then alert, with tail raised in alarm, they look magnificent. However, this time we kept our distance and they continued their dignified but relentless journey north. Caribou always seem to be on the move, maybe slowly, but always moving.

So we watched, spellbound, as the sinuous lines faded, ghost-like, into the white emptiness of the Barrens, the females carrying the future of the herd in their bellies. It struck us as an optimistic gesture, a hint of spring on a cold winter's day, those graceful animals heading out into that awesome infinity of snow and ice. It could be true what they say – eternity is white, not black.

ISLAND OF THE WAKING BEARS

'Far north, in the foggy regions of the Arctic, there lie some mountainous islands. A gale-ridden sea, hundreds of miles wide, separates them from the nearest mainland, and the forces of nature, in all their strength, have free play around them. From the north and east the polar ice exerts its pressure, and every autumn the ice attacks and, together with the cold, the snowstorms and the polar night, lays siege to the islands, folding them in its chill embrace.'

So wrote an early explorer of the group of islands known as Svalbard, 'the land with the cold coast'. Placed as they are some 3000 kilometres north of London and only 1200 kilometres from the North Pole, the coast is indeed cold, the sea being frozen for all but four months of the year.

It was 4 March 1984 and we were just setting off from Svalbard's capital on a six-week expedition to film polar bears. Our overloaded sledge had overturned on a steep snow bank, watched by several local residents who, I suspect, thought we would not make it. They were driving in trucks, we four were on skidoos, dragging seven sledges between us, heading for the distant island of Edgeöya, some 200 kilometres to the east. As we had only travelled one kilometre, the possibility that we wouldn't make it also crossed our minds.

There was considerable interest in our expedition, for few people set off on a six-week trip in early March, Svalbard's coldest month, and even fewer are ever granted permission to cross the sea ice to the island of Edgeöya, a nature reserve with severely restricted access. An expedition by the Norsk Polar Institute two years previously had identified the island as an important breeding area for polar bears and one of the members of that expedition, and ours, was Oslo-based Rasmus Hansson, a Norwegian whose experience with bears and polar exploration was extensive. Equally experienced was the other Norwegian in our team, Birger Amundsen, and he had also worked extensively with bears in Svalbard. So Mike and I, protected by such able guides, felt very confident of the outcome of our expedition.

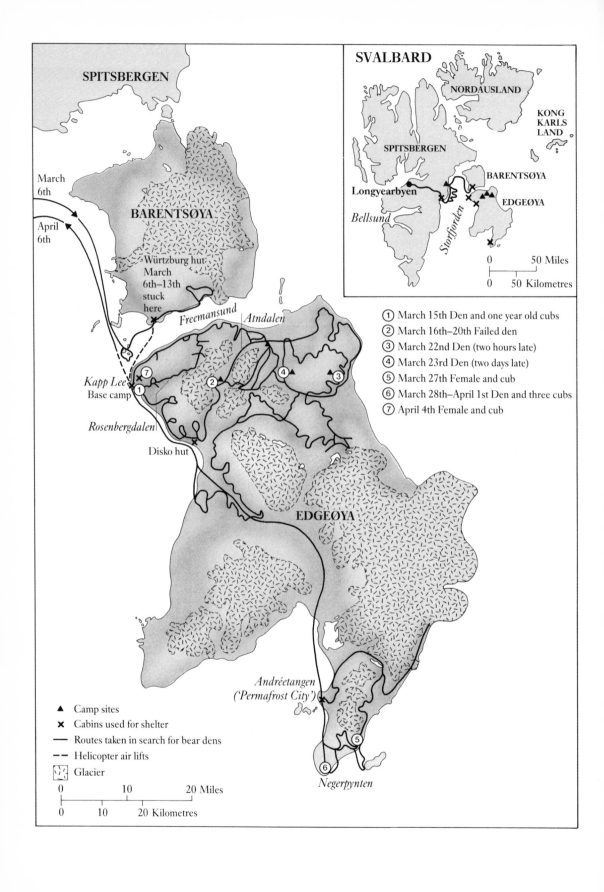

SPITSBERGEN

BARENTSØYA

March 6th

April 6th

Würtzburg hut
March 6th–13th stuck here

Freemansund   *Atndalen*

Kapp Lee
Base camp

Rosenbergdalen

Disko hut

EDGEØYA

Andréetangen
('Permafrost City')

Negerpynten

SVALBARD

NORDAUSLAND

KONG KARLS LAND

SPITSBERGEN

BARENTSØYA

Longyearbyen

EDGEØYA

Bellsund

Storfjorden

0   50 Miles

0   50 Kilometres

① March 15th Den and one year old cubs
② March 16th–20th Failed den
③ March 22nd Den (two hours late)
④ March 23rd Den (two days late)
⑤ March 27th Female and cub
⑥ March 28th–April 1st Den and three cubs
⑦ April 4th Female and cub

▲ Camp sites
✕ Cabins used for shelter
— Routes taken in search for bear dens
- - Helicopter air lifts
▨ Glacier

0   10   20 Miles

0   10   20 Kilometres

However, we were in no doubt of the risks of the trip, both financial and physical, for conditions would be unrelentingly harsh and we might not even be able to cross the sea ice with our heavy sledges. When and if we reached the island, we would then have to find an active polar bear den, and that is nearly always difficult.

Rasmus and Birger had described the problem. Female polar bears leave the sea ice in the autumn, and head inland, finding a suitable snow bank high up in the mountains. They then dig out a den and let the snow blow over the entrance, sealing themselves in against the cold. Having been mated by a male bear out on the summer ice, the females give birth to one or two cubs at about Christmas. They nurse them until the weak sun returns in mid to late March, then, responding to the light, break open the den and within a few days lead the cubs down from the mountains and out onto the sea ice to hunt for seals.

It was the brief period of activity, when the female breaks out of the den with her cubs, that we wished to film – a crucial sequence for the marine film but one of the most difficult of any wildlife sequence in the world. Mike and I had discussed long and hard how best to achieve this and decided that two teams would minimise the physical risks and maximise our chance of success. So the four of us had everything we needed to film and survive for six weeks, including as much fuel as we could carry. We would be totally isolated from other humans. Our sledges, but not our minds, groaned under the burden.

We righted the overturned sledge and motored on, soon leaving our entourage behind. Longyearbyen, the capital of Svalbard, became a memory. We had spent the last three days there, gathering food, organising equipment, packing sledges, and now we were keen to press on. It was 4 March, an important day, for it was the first time the sun had climbed above the horizon for 110 days. Its appearance over the mountains struck us as a symbol of hope – spring was on the way.

Our route to the east led us through a wide valley, flanked on either side by rounded mountains, smoothed by the winter snows. The sun was already setting, turning the mountains pink – it was just 2 p.m. Feeding in the valley were scattered groups of reindeer, and like the caribou in the Barrens of Canada, they were chipping through the snow crust to reach the lichens beneath; the scene was very beautiful.

Travelling by skidoo, wrapped in numerous layers of clothes, masked against the frosty wind, deafened by the roar of the engine, the mind becomes isolated from your fellow travellers. However, on reflection, I know we were all feeling the same – a sense of anticipation, excitement, adventure, a little overawed and apprehensive perhaps, but, even though it was −28°C and darkness was falling, we all felt lucky to be there.

The valley separated to east and west, and we headed east, up into the mountains. Our problems did not start until we reached the glacier that lay across our path. The twilight of night was upon us and the next three hours proved to be a sweaty struggle. We floundered in deep snow, manhauled loads, righted overturned sledges, burnt out drive belts on the skidoos, looped back and forth to drag the sledges over the pass, roped them through narrow gaps in the moraines and over the mountain top. But, largely unscathed, we made it to the far side, and all this activity certainly kept us warm. We all regretted not seeing the nearby glacier in the darkness, but on the return journey were able to admire it in the glow of a spring night. The spectacular walls of green ice and windswept snow and the rocky and tortuous track through the moraine made us realise why we had struggled that dark night with our overloaded sledges.

Once over the pass, it was plain sailing on the flats of the ice-covered valley floor. All Mike and I did was follow the red reflectors of Rasmus and Birger's skidoos for what seemed hour after hour. We were grateful for their previous experience, for just when we thought we had missed Agaard cabin in the blackness of the night, we found it in the headlights. This little trapper's hut lay on the edge of the frozen sea but there was little to see, for snow drifts obliterated all bar the roof. But once the little stove was lit, food simmering and sleeping bags laid out, it made a cosy roost and for a first night out in this beautiful country it was memorable. We unpacked the sledges under the glorious glow of the Aurora Borealis. The atmospheric flares streaked and shimmered from one horizon to another, drifting across the stars at midnight. The Aurora was brighter than the moon, and we stood enthralled in the icy air – sleep came easily that night.

After the days of planning, packing and travel we woke reluctantly. We had been warm in our sleeping bags but were pleased it had been a cold night, for we hoped the sea-ice in Storfjorden was solid. Just as we headed out towards the island of Edgeöya we were seen by our first bear, a big male who came across the ice to check us out. Before the camera could be released from the sledges, he took fright and ran off: a disappointment – and a relief, for we were still tuned to the streets of Bristol and with our heads full of the stories of aggressive killer bears we were not ready for a full-scale confrontation. It was good to see that at least one bear was frightened of humans.

Full of optimism, we headed due east across the frozen sea, but after five kilometres were confronted by an impenetrable jumble of broken ice. We tried to pick our way through this tortured landscape but eventually reached a lead of water which had only just refrozen. Considering it unsafe, we reluctantly turned north to try the long route round the head of the bay. It would add a day to our journey, but despite the beckoning peaks of Edgeöya on the eastern horizon, we failed to force a way through the pack ice.

Darkness closed around us quickly that day, so we headed for shore, setting up the tents on the sea ice, the only flattish place around. As we did so we saw five more bears, and set the trip-wire system around tents and sledges carefully. The theory is that when a bear comes to investigate, the trip-wire sets off a thunderflash. This frightens the bear and also wakes us up, so if the bear should return, we would be able to defend ourselves.

However, that night was extremely cold, and after a preliminary doze, I lay half conscious, with bones chilled to the marrow. Suddenly I was very much awake, aware of the footsteps of a bear just outside the tent. Not sure whether Mike was awake, I whispered my fears to him and we lay there and

listened – another creak in the snow, and another. He agreed there was a bear
stalking closer. We made the rifle ready by our sides, realising that if it charged
it would be on us before the trip-wire did its work, for in the darkness we had
set it too close to our tent. The creaks continued spasmodically – the bear was
still there and our ears strained to hear it breathing – our hearts beat faster as
we lay there freezing and frightened. We decided the fear was irrational and
we had better sleep, but just as we dozed off another series of creaks re-alerted
us to the threat. Thus the minutes and hours passed by until we finally decided
that our imaginations had run riot in the darkness, and the noises were merely
the sea ice cracking under the tent. Thus reassured we slept soundly until
dawn. On reflection it amuses me that we were not concerned about the ice.
Only the polar bear looms large in the wild dreams of Arctic adventurers.

We packed the sledges in the glow from the sunrise over the distant
mountains of Edgeöya. It was only 7 a.m. – spring was returning fast and we
left hurriedly. Our route was still barred by impenetrable pack ice so we
looped north, finding smooth going at the head of the bay. We roared past
several stunning icebergs, glowing green and blue in the sunshine, and were
relieved to find the head of the bay passable – open water often bars travellers
at that spot. We continued to motor relentlessly on, hour after hour. But upon
reaching Freemansund we found our way barred yet again by pack ice.
Encouraged by the sight of Kapp Lee, the site of our intended camp, six
kilometres away, we manhauled skidoos and sledges through the jumble,
and out of crevasses, but struggle as we did, we could not reach our elusive
goal and had to back-track to a little cabin Rasmus knew of on Barentsöya.
Darkness was descending as we approached, and after ten hours of travel and
chill, and several disappointments, we could not believe what we saw. A
hungry bear had destroyed the front of the cabin, rummaged inside, and left it
open to the elements. It was now packed with ice and snow, right to the roof.

Reluctant to pitch tents in the dark, particularly after the previous night's
chilly experiences, we started clearing the hut and within three hours we were
inside and most of the snow was outside. We patched up the window and
door, set the trip-wires and made a meal, then snuggled down amongst the
cramped remnants of snow and equipment – it had been an eventful day.

The next seven days proved far from eventful, for we couldn't reach our
destination. Storms and mild weather ensured the open water in Freemansund
continued to bar our route to Edgeöya, and we paced back and forth along the
ice edge in frustration.

Hoping the sea would refreeze, we killed time by filming several hardy
little reindeer scraping lichens off the rocks – there was little else for them to
eat. We were visited by a bear and her yearling cub, unfortunately when we
were sleeping, for we were keen to film her. She set off the trip-wire which
protected the hut, which woke us and alarmed them. All we saw was their
rapid departure over the hill. They were the only bears we saw in seven days
searching – not an encouraging sign. The first seabirds arrived from the south,
fulmars and black guillemots, and we filmed their courtship in the pale yellow
sunshine of a cold spring day. Several ringed seals snorted disgust at our

presence. They welcomed the open water, we did not. Growing anxious at the loss of time, we eventually got through on the radio and booked a helicopter airlift. We had hesitated because of the great expense involved, but now our whole expedition might fail if we delayed much longer.

In the event, it was another four days before the stormy weather abated and allowed the helicopter to reach us, but as Birger and I flew the first leg across to our intended base camp at Kapp Lee, it was clear that the yawning gaps in the ice and the extensive chaos of jagged ice blocks would have held us up for a lot longer.

The helicopter could only lift two skidoos or sledges at a time, so the plan was for Birger and I to open up the field station hut and establish base camp whilst the helicopter ferried back and forth. When we reached Kapp Lee we found ourselves thwarted once again, for a bear had broken the substantial door and left it slightly open. No problem you might think, but the gap had allowed snow to blow in and fill the area behind – this had then frozen. All we could get through the gap was an arm, but after two hours using this to chip away with an ice axe we were no nearer opening the door. The wind was now blowing hard, we were getting cold, and darkness was closing in, so we reluctantly broke in through the window, then cut the ice away from inside.

Once inside we were relieved to see that the bear had not wrecked the sleeping accommodation, and within an hour we had a fire going and a meal cooking. After a ten-day journey we were finally set up to start work in earnest – we had lost valuable time but were in good spirits. As I snuggled down in the top bunk that night, I noticed the scratches of a previous visitor carved in the ceiling. It was the great claw marks of a bear – I had sweet dreams that night.

14 March was foul, blowing hard from the north, overcast, bad visibility and cold, a day to attend to the film equipment and remove some of the snow from inside the hut. But by late afternoon the storm had passed and we watched a red sun set behind the distant mountains of Spitsbergen. Its warm glow turned the snow-covered cliffs behind us pink, and the open leads in the ice in front of the cabin reflected its colourful departure. The air was now very cold, and the comparatively warm sea-water steamed. Great green and blue icebergs lay trapped offshore and we admired their angular beauty. We were accompanied by a friend, an arctic fox that had befriended us and was now inseparable. We christened him or her 'Lief', and it soon learnt that to respond to the call of that name meant a reward of a few raisins or bits of biscuit. Lief became hand tame within half an hour, and was a charming mascot throughout our stay. All five of us watched the sun go down together that night.

Next day was cold, −27°C, but as it was calm and clear we were soon off on our first search for bear dens. Mike and Birger left a few moments ahead of Rasmus and me, for they were going to search some mountainsides further to the south, whilst we did a circuit of the hills nearer to camp, a round trip of about 70 kilometres. We had organised the expedition with the idea of splitting into two teams, to maximise our search for bears with the minimum of risk. But we still had a very difficult task ahead of us, and were surprised to find Mike and Birger stopped only two kilometres down the coast, their excited signalling indicating that they had already found a den. The hole was clearly visible in a snow bank at the top of a sea cliff, and they had seen a female bear disappear into it. We didn't know whether she had cubs but it was a likely possibility. We could not believe our luck – a den just five minutes from base camp, discovered on day one. It was too good to be true, and Rasmus and I soon had a ledge cut into a snow bank some 70 metres from the den, and a hide made out of snow blocks.

I had suggested to Mike and Birger that they should hide until we were also hidden and ready to film, the plan being to use the noisy departure of their skidoos as a decoy. With the lens lined up on the den entrance, we signalled them with the walkie-talkies, and the plan worked like a charm. The moment they started to depart, a bear's head appeared and watched the skidoos, until she considered them distant enough to come back out into the sun. She did indeed have cubs for a second head emerged, and at this magic moment Mike was looking back and had his own thoughts on the event.

'From about a kilometre away it seemed safe to slow down and glance back towards the den. I could just see two cubs sliding about above the entrance. In my mind I could hear Hugh's camera purring away behind the snow shelter, at last recording the sort of scenes that we had all imagined during these two weeks of mixed fortune. The cubs looked well-fed, perhaps larger than I had expected, but it was clearly a family den because I could now see an even bigger head, which I took to be the mother, peering out of the den entrance.

'The scene was not much more than a fleeting impression, but it stayed with me vividly for the rest of the day. As we headed southwards, away from the bears, I found myself wondering whether we were almost too lucky to find such a good den so close to our base camp. I wasn't surprised when, at our first stop, Birger expressed a similar nagging doubt about what we had seen. He also thought the large cubs had moved about very confidently on the steep slope, which could mean that they had been out of the den for twelve days or so. If this was the case, it might also indicate a very early season and the possibility that we wouldn't find any dens at the first stages of break-out. However, the exhilarating thought that Hugh might, at that very minute, be filming a memorable sequence, pushed pessimism out of my mind.'

Pessimism was actually appropriate, for when I looked through the camera as they climbed out of the den, I realised that there *was* something wrong; the cubs were too big. I had seen photographs of three-month-old polar bear cubs but those I could see through my lens seemed too big: perhaps it was a trick of the light? Rasmus whispered in my ear and confirmed my suspicions. They were one-year-old cubs, a bit of a disappointment, but still a delight.

Emerging from their den, the cubs slid about in the snow and were joined by the female. They wandered off to the north, out of sight behind a rock bluff, then five minutes later returned at a run, dived into the den, and despite what proved to be a very chilly wait, did not reappear until we gave up at dusk. Meanwhile, Mike and Birger were searching the mountains to the south.

Above: Birger with 'Lief', the arctic fox, and Rasmus with his breakfast at −36°C

Right: crossing the sea ice to Edgeöya

Below: looking for a way across Freemansund

Below right: stranded here on Barentsöya for nine days

Rasmus checking a bear den just below him

'We imagined that Hugh and Rasmus already had some good film "in the can", and by the time we turned away from the edge of the sea ice towards the first sizeable valley, we were in good spirits to start the search for alternative dens. It wasn't until two hours later, when we were still only halfway up what appeared to be a tiny valley on the map, that the size of the task became clear. Compared to the distant horizons of the sea ice, this winding indentation into the hills had at first seemed relatively small-scale, sheltered, almost friendly. We had split up to search either side of the steep-sided valley, and Birger now looked like an insignificant black ant crawling along the opposite slope, high above the wide valley floor. The scenery had a grandeur which both inspired and humbled. Although in many places the snow cover was very thin and icy, there were also endless side gullies and sheltered slopes where the snow was thick enough to conceal a denning bear.

'We stopped frequently to scan with binoculars for any signs of bear prints on the slopes, or for a lump of snow which could be the plug from a den entrance pushed out by a mother bear. We also had to keep a careful watch for shadowy areas of pure ice, on which the skidoo loses all grip, and for deep hidden gullies down which a plunge would doubtless end for ever any further exploration in this exquisite frozen landscape.

'We continued such searches all day without success in four other valleys, until the pastel shades of an Arctic sunset faded into an ice-blue twilight, forcing us to head back towards Kapp Lee where we looked forward with anticipation to news from Hugh and Rasmus. The news was not good and obviously Birger and myself were disappointed to hear that the den wasn't quite what was wanted. However, because yearling cubs in a den had not been filmed before, it was agreed that Hugh and Rasmus would put in one more day's film effort while we searched further away for an alternative location. Sleep came very easily that night as the fire lost its heat and the washing-up water froze solid amongst the dirty plates and pans.

'Friday 16 March was a beautifully calm, clear morning with the temperature a reasonable – 16°C as we left Hugh and Rasmus to their long vigil at the yearling den and set off round the shadowy bulk of Kapp Lee headland before veering eastwards along the south shore of Freemansund. For the first 15 kilometres or so the gaps between jumbled piles of broken sea ice and the steep cliffs were sometimes only just wide enough for a skidoo and sledge to pass. A grotesquely-shaped, crystal landscape, where a wandering ice bear could be expected at any moment. In fact, to our great surprise, we saw only one bear all day.

'After a couple of hours' difficult travelling, the cliffs turned into rounded hills and fell back from the shore. Now we were able to get higher and search all the tiny valleys up the coast as far as Walter Thyman's Bukta. At times on our left we had the most spectacular views of Freemansund with its great mass of ice floes moving along on the tide, and the island of Barentsöya beyond. This "plan" view made us realise why we hadn't been able to find a way across a week ago. By 5 p.m. we had travelled 80 kilometres without even a sign of any bear tracks, let alone a den opening. In one place we disturbed a flock of ptarmigan in brilliant white plumage which took off like a snow flurry to land higher up the hill. A surprising number of creamy-coloured Svalbard reindeer wandered in small groups on the open hillsides, scraping away thin layers of snow with their wide hooves to get at the saxifrage buds and lichens below. With their short, stocky legs and long shaggy hair they looked more like large mountain sheep than deer. There was certainly life in this harsh Arctic landscape, but a shortage of polar bears, it seemed.

'The sun had dipped below the mountain, casting Atnadalen into deep luminous shadow by the time we were still two hours from base. This long valley led us from the east coast through the hills to the west and thence back to Kapp Lee – a 250-kilometre circular route. I was beginning to fantasise about food, warmth and a rest from skidoo noise when suddenly Birger raised his hand, cautioning me to stop and turn off the engine. His excellent eyes had spotted a bear walking high up on the eastern side of the valley. Judging from the size and thin shape we felt sure she was a female. The slope was so steep at this point it seemed amazing that she could walk along it with such confidence and without sliding down to join us on the valley floor. The twilight made it difficult now to pick out any distinguishing features on the snow slope, so that when she stopped, put her head down and completely disappeared, we hardly dared believe that we had perhaps found another maternity den.

'We drove our skidoos to the foot of the hillside underneath the spot where we had last seen her. In this half-light not even the merest hint of a hole nor any footprints could be seen above. It was as if we were witness to some strange conjuring trick of the far north, thought up by the trolls. Nevertheless, without feeling overconfident, we marked the place with massive footprint arrows in the snow and set off on the cold, and by now almost dark, two-hour run back to Kapp Lee, where Hugh and Rasmus were already cooking supper in a nicely-warmed hut.'

We packed hastily at dawn, with Rasmus and I roping enough onto the sledges to camp close to the female bear for several nights if necessary. Lief clambered about on the loads, receiving titbits for providing amusing photos, then suddenly fled, with tail between legs. We wondered what we had done to cause the alarm, then suddenly became aware of a large male bear marching purposefully into camp — too close for comfort. Mike grabbed a rifle whilst I dashed into the cabin for a thunderflash, but the sudden burst of activity frightened the bear and it lumbered off into the ice floes — we were relieved.

We travelled south together, past spectacular sea cliffs, crowned by rock pinnacles, echoes of gothic spires, towering up into the mist. Fulmars flew amongst them, prospecting for nest sites. We passed Disko cabin, then headed up the wide valley of Atnadalen, climbing high into the mountains. The den site was about 20 kilometres inland from the coast, and we reached it in about an hour and a half, manoeuvring through a glacial moraine on the way.

When we reached what Mike thought was the spot there was nothing to see, not a footprint, no den entrance, nothing. We wondered if it was the right place, and even climbed the mountainside to see if the den was visible from

Above: the end of a day's searching for bears

Left: inside Kapp Lee cabin

Previous page: our friend 'Lief' and a typical valley on Edgeöya

33

above. But blowing snow had obliterated all the signs that the female might have left when she walked the slope yesterday.

She had disappeared into the mountainside like a ghost, so a den must be there somewhere. Mike and Birger wondered if they had been dreaming, but we set up camp on the mountainside regardless, some 70 metres from where they thought the den might be. We built igloo-type walls to screen us from the bear's gaze and the cruel wind, bade Mike and Birger farewell, and settled down for a long wait.

Sunday 18 March proved to be a stormy night, with strong wind and snow. My diary records the events of the next day. 'Didn't sleep well – tent flapping, too noisy. Up at 6.30 a.m. and at 6.45 a.m. there is a bear, out of the den where Mike had expected. She had a short stroll, then back in. Couldn't film her as still quite dark, and snow blowing into lens. Her head out at 10 a.m. and 11 a.m., looking around, yawning, and looking at us! Manage to film appearance shot we want. A thrill to be succeeding at last and how inspiring it is to see a bear's head appear out of a mountainside – it will make quite a start to the film series. But there is no sign of cubs yet. At 3.30 p.m. five reindeer walk down the mountain past the den – she watches them closely – they leap off in alarm when they notice her beady black eyes and nose. It will make a nice sequence in the wind-blown snow. Temp. dropped all day from −3 to −15°C. By nightfall I'm grateful for the cosy tent and sleeping bag.'

On Monday she seemed very shy. All we saw until 5 p.m. was a nose, and that only briefly. Then she climbed out, stretched, circled, and clambered back in through the narrow hole, leaving a back leg waving amusingly in the air. It was great to see a complete bear, for it had been a long, cold wait. The temperature was −23°C and frostbite threatened all day. We radioed Mike and Birger, asking them for more supplies tomorrow and confirmed we had a denning female on the hill above us and that it would only be a matter of days before the sequence was in the bag. It was a real treat for Birger's birthday, and we wondered whether he and Mike had also had a good day.

'Monday 19 March was one of those clear, still days when despite the cold the Arctic takes on a face of pristine, almost immaculate beauty. The evocative calls of the first few kittiwakes to arrive from the south added to the sense of well-being as Birger and I set out from Disko hut with the sun on our faces. The conditions were perfect for a long day's search but suddenly, only 300 metres away, Birger's skidoo came to an expensive-sounding halt. The rest of the day was spent fetching the necessary spares from Kapp Lee and struggling to replace the broken rear suspension parts without suffering frostbitten fingers.

'It was dark, windy and snowing again by the time we set up the radio aerial for our 9 p.m. schedule. We found that the batteries had got too cold to power the set, so it was a waste of time anyway. To add to the list of failures, the pump we had brought to transfer the last few litres of precious fuel from the large drums was seized solid. As a gesture of defiance, we poured a tot of whisky each and started the night shift – myself as mechanic and Birger on supper duty.

'After a long day without a proper meal, the smell of tinned army goulash seemed unbelievably good. Birger turned proudly from the stove bearing the steaming pan, but before reaching the table he somehow lost his grip and dropped the whole thing on the floor, from where it sent up a shower of high-velocity meat and veg! It would have been difficult to tell anguish from laughter as we scraped warm lumps of goulash from ceiling, walls and clothing like two demented, half-starved prisoners. I was glad to have almost had my fill in this bizarre manner before Birger pointed out that the inside of the hut still looked horribly as if some very ill person had vomited explosively in every direction! The long, restful sleep needed after such a day came to an end at 6 a.m. the following morning when a large male bear stumbled into the trip-wire surrounding our skidoos outside and set off one of the flare pots with a sharp explosion. It sent him running away in an undignified wobbling of massive backside.'

Rasmus and I also had a visitor that night. It was 5.30 a.m. when I woke to the footsteps of a bear approaching the tent. She had come to check us out. I woke Rasmus and we lay there, completely cocooned in sleeping bags, powerless to do anything. In the stillness of the night all you hear is your heart – which beats a little faster – and the crunch of the bear's footsteps just outside. She approached to within 20 metres or so, but we had no real fear, as denning females are very cautious, and would rather defend their cubs than risk an attack. However, she would be very hungry after four months without food, and could no doubt smell the lingering aroma of our supper. We were relieved when after three approaches to the tent, she returned to her den.

On Monday night, she woke us at 3.30 a.m., and this time her approach was more purposeful. Last night we slept with the rifle under the bed, this time it was on the bed, and ready for action. Feeling more threatened, Rasmus shouted a vehement oath in Norwegian – probably an impolite version of 'go away, bear' for after a brief pause she rapidly departed, padding back to the den at a run. Later, we heard her walk past once more, then nothing.

We were greeted at dawn by heavy snow, and sat for six hours in the blizzard without a sign of her. This was no real surprise to Rasmus as his previous experience with denning bears suggested that they wisely prefer calm sunny days in which to wander from the den. We had not seen cubs yet either, but the females usually break out a couple of days before them, so we were still optimistic. The family might stay in the area for anything up to twenty-five days, but the average is fourteen. The hungry females are torn between hurrying to the ice to hunt seals, or letting their cubs develop in the safety of the mountains. She has a lot to lose, for most polar bears have cubs only once every three years, the offspring depending on her guidance for over two years. In any event, the sea ice is a dangerous place, for male bears will kill and eat cubs. This is the theory put forward as the reason why denning areas are traditional, and remote from the main bear populations.

So Rasmus and I felt we had nothing to fear from her non-appearance. But as the hours slipped by, we grew more and more anxious, and some

*Dangerous
conditions
for skidooing*

*Far left: large
male bear*

37

instinct suggested she was no longer hidden in the mountainside above us. Eventually our patience cracked, and Rasmus gingerly climbed up to the den. With pistol at the ready, he peered inside, and not only was she not there, but the lack of scratch marks on the roof of the den showed she had not had cubs; she was a rare failed breeder, and we cursed our bad luck.

Anxious now at the loss of five days in the peak of the denning period, we struck camp as quickly as possible and tried to head off Mike and Birger who would be coming with fresh supplies. We wanted to save them a cold journey, and save some of our precious fuel. At least the activity of packing equipment and sledges warmed us up and helped to distract us from the bitter disappointment we both felt. We could only be philosophical and just keep trying, but the journey out of the mountains was not a joyful one.

After an hour's motoring we met Mike and Birger in the pack ice beyond Disko cabin and the meeting was most welcome after four days of isolation. They too were disappointed at our news, and we at theirs, for their skidoo trouble had left them with little time for searching and they had found nothing new. As we retreated north to Kapp Lee we saw the first kittiwakes prospecting their colony and this tangible sign of spring caused increased anxiety over the lost time. However, the evening was convivial and the open fire warm and welcome. Waiting by the camera for four days had proved a very cold experience.

21 March was a day of perfect Arctic spring, and ptarmigan display calls echoed off the cliffs above the cabin as we set off on another long search. We slithered over mountainsides all day, but found no sign of bears. We set up camp on the northern edge of Atnadalen, having arranged to meet Mike and Birger there to compare notes. When darkness fell and they had still not arrived we began to worry. Then at 9 p.m. they at last appeared with no news of bears, but with stories of breakdowns, accidents and navigational errors. Although they were too exhausted to go into detail there and then, it seemed there was a need to read between the lines, for Mike woke us at night shouting in nightmare sleep, 'Don't go near the edge.' Next morning he described their eventful day.

'When we left on the morning of 21 March, myself and Birger planned to take a longer route south, via Diskobukta Bay, before turning east to cross the centre of the island. As with any search there is always the hope that new territory will reveal fresh bounty and I certainly felt full of optimism as we entered the previously unexplored valley of Smelledalen on that glorious crisp morning. The light was perfect for spotting bear tracks or den entrances in the snow. To begin with, the valley was impressively wide, but narrowed after six kilometres or so as it climbed between the mountains towards the distant glacier of Storskavlen. Following our usual search pattern we had taken a side each, and enjoyed the exhilaration of exploring a small winding side valley of breathtaking beauty. In all likelihood, no human had ever been up there before, although numerous fox and reindeer tracks showed that I wasn't entirely alone in this rare privilege.

'I suppose it was just over half an hour before I re-emerged into the main valley, having enjoyed myself but not found any sign of bears. Now it was Birger whom I couldn't see, although there was a dark valley leading up to a tongue of the glacier that I imagined he would be exploring. Looking more carefully, I could just pick out a skidoo track disappearing over the brow of a far snow bank, but something told me I ought to wait for his reappearance rather than disappearing up another valley myself.

'Forty minutes passed and I began to feel anxious: a great silence hung over the mountainsides: nothing moved except an occasional swirl of dry snow crystals lifted by a hidden wind from high on the opposite ridge – backlit, shimmering. I felt an intense moment of isolation and, it must be admitted, a sense of the smallness and frailty of human life in such a vast, unforgiving environment. But then, suddenly, my mood was broken. A tiny figure caught my attention high up near the distant glacier and with binoculars I could see that Birger was waving his arms above his head in the prearranged signal that meant, "Join me over here as soon as possible – I've found a bear" or "I need help!" As I reached him I could see that, on this occasion, assistance was required.

'Birger recounted how he had gone up the valley as far as he could and then started a downhill turn to come back. But the mountainside here had almost blown clear of snow, and in the shade was mostly covered by a treacherous glaze of ice on which his loaded sledge and skidoo had begun to slip sideways down the increasingly steep slope, ending up in its present position, on the very edge of a sheer drop into a snow-filled chasm whose bottom we couldn't see and didn't particularly want to think about! Birger, with a wry, unruffled Norwegian grin, told me that he was on the point of jumping off to save his life when, by good fortune, the skidoo had wedged against the one sizeable rock on an otherwise smooth surface.

'We needed every bit of rope we had with us to reach from Birger's precariously-balanced skidoo to mine, 40 metres higher up on the nearest patch of reasonable snow. Once the towline was fixed I signalled to Birger and we both revved our engines to full power simultaneously. With relief I felt his skidoo following, albeit in a pendulous arc, which I trusted wasn't taking him too near the brink. I dared not look back, however, for it was essential to concentrate hard and keep as much forward momentum as possible. If Birger's skidoo went over the edge now it would inevitably pull mine with it.

'After a tow of perhaps 150 metres I could feel the rope slacken, telling me with relief that Birger was finding enough decent grip himself to get out of danger. Just when I thought we had the problem cracked, my own skidoo reached a glistening area of ice and itself started sliding sideways down the steep angle at an alarming rate. I desperately steered for a patch where small stones were sticking through the surface, but when the skidoo reached them it didn't merely stop – it bucked and started to roll over.

'The next few seconds are a blurred recollection of sky, ground and machine, tumbling, whirring, bouncing – over and over – until somehow I was on my back with the skidoo just below, the right way up, its engine gently

Overleaf:
adult male bear

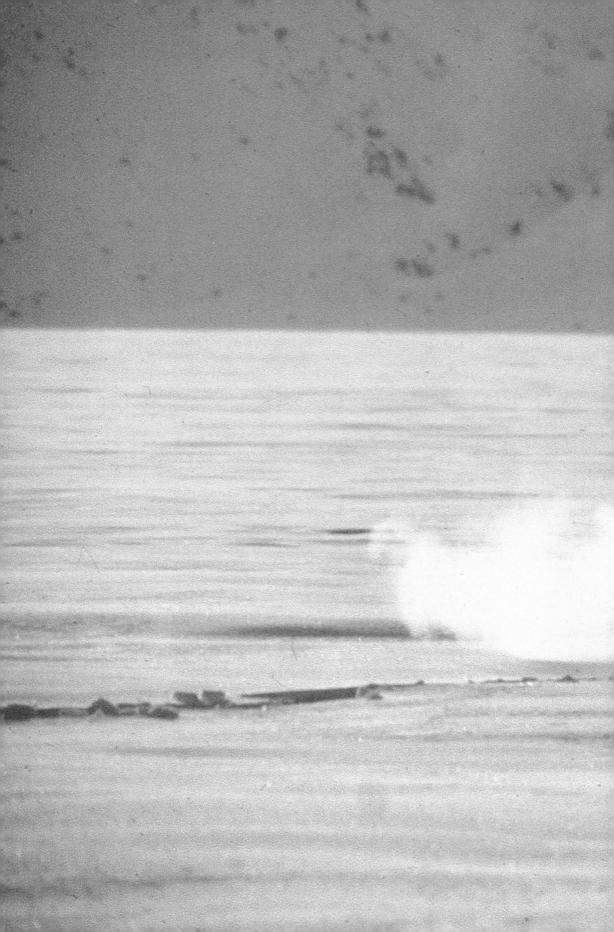

ticking over and minus only a few bits of windshield! On one gyration I'd felt the weight of the machine (about the same as a large motorbike) bounce on my leg and now hardly dared move for fear of discovering a broken ankle. Luck was with us, however. It was certainly a bit tender but thankfully only bruised, and we were glad to get back to the valley floor without any further trouble.'

When Rasmus and I left Mike and Birger at dawn on 22 March, we spent three days searching the whole of the north-eastern part of Edgeöya. Late on the first afternoon we found the first sign of cubs in a beautiful little combe on the south side of Kuitra, meaning 'the valley of the peep-peep river'. But we had missed them by just an hour or two and were full of regret. What fantastic film it would have made – slides, day beds, lots of walks, a temporary but obviously well-used den – all in the loveliest setting, with snow-covered hills rolling off over the far horizon.

Their tracks led over a range of hills so we set up camp on the other side in the hope of intercepting them on their way to the sea ice at dawn. I climbed the hills at dusk and looked for the bears, but there was nothing but snow and ice. The frozen sea lay motionless below. To the east the next land was the far coast of Siberia and alone up there, surrounded by that empty wilderness, I felt complete fulfilment. Today we had probably gazed on land that no human had ever seen before. I was lucky to be there and, successful or not, was enjoying every moment of the experience.

It was a stormy night. There was lots of wind and snow, and the dawn was very cloudy, with bad visibility. We packed up camp and had one last look for the mother and cubs, but had to admit we'd missed them. Disappointed, we travelled up Pistradalen, 'the valley of the squeaking river', into a dangerous 'white-out'. Rasmus found his way with compass-bearing precision, avoiding snow gullies and icy traps, whilst I looked for bears. At about 1 p.m., in foul weather, I spotted a den on the east side of Pistradalen. There were droppings, two entrances and footprints. Everything looked hopeful, but as we built our big snow shelter we became ever more doubtful, for there was no sign of the bear. We found it difficult to accept the disappointment of being late at two consecutive dens, but finished the perfect igloo-style hide, in case our senses were wrong.

Next morning we'd had no sighting of the bear, so Rasmus went up the mountainside to the hole and discovered that it had indeed been a maternity den, but female and cubs had left maybe two days before. We had to stomach yet another big disappointment, and such a feeling is like physical sickness. However, determined to succeed, we quickly packed camp and did a long search of the northern part of the island before heading back to Kapp Lee.

We had covered 228 kilometres in four days and seen just one bear, but on the way home we met two big males, one a really superb animal who stood on his hind legs and towered above us as we approached, then backed off into the pack ice. The other suddenly surprised us on a ridge just above the skidoos. He was blooded and determined and we wondered if he had fought with the other male. Such fights can be vicious if the prize is a female bear in heat. He followed us and had to be disuaded with two flares. But each time he came forward again and in the end it was us who had to back off! Within half an hour we were back home at Kapp Lee. Perhaps it was one of those big male bears that woke us at 5.30 a.m. by banging into our trip-wires, but at least he ran off.

Next day, apart from the delight of a thorough wash, we had some hard thinking to do. It was already 25 March and we had taken very little film. Time was running out. We had searched all the area on the northern part of the island and it seemed that ice conditions in the autumn of 1983 were to blame for the lack of bears. Apparently the sea ice did not freeze to the north-east of Edgeöya until November, so the natural migration of pregnant females from the permanent ice could not take place until very late.

We now regretted the lack of access to the world's finest denning area, Kong Karls Land, just 150 kilometres to the north. Rasmus and Birger had studied bears there and found densities of up to twenty maternity dens in a square kilometre. However, most of the Arctic's denning areas are more like Edgeöya, with large areas of barren ground between each den. The only place we had not searched was the southern part of the island, very remote from base camp. So it was with a mixture of reluctance and optimism that we headed south with seven days' supplies and a sledge load of fuel.

The journey was extremely difficult, for it was very windy, creating not only extreme cold, but a complete white-out. We all used compasses but, even though on exactly the right route, nearly plunged to our deaths into a crevasse which lay hidden in our path. After that we collected the black droppings of reindeer, and walked in front of the leading skidoo throwing the dark markers ahead. If the dropping disappeared, there was a precipice or crevasse. Thus we made slow but safe progress and eventually crossed over the mountain pass.

The rest of the run was long but easy, and the low sun and blowing snow amongst the pack ice made for some memorable film. We were delighted to find the cabin at Andrée Tangan had not been wrecked by bears, but the sight on opening the door was stunning. Every surface, tables, chairs, books, and bunks were covered in several centimetres of hoar-frost. It looked like a fairy-tale world and it seemed appropriate that our scientific adviser, Thor Larsen, had christened the hut 'Permafrost City'.

With numerous logs available on the nearby shore, we soon changed the interior from Arctic chill to tropical damp, but by next morning the Arctic had lost some of its glamour, for the temperature had dropped to −31°C. It has been said that the pleasures of the Arctic at this time of the year are aesthetic rather than physical and during ten hours of searching the cold wind was almost unbearable, with frostbite threatening nose and face and watering eyes freezing up.

At 4 p.m. we thought our luck had finally changed, for Rasmus and I found a mother and cub on a snow slope above the sea ice. The cub was playing, climbing up the steep hill and sliding down, colliding with its resting mother. I stalked closer, using an iceberg for cover, then just as I was in position for some good film, mother and cub fled onto the sea ice. I was

Above: skidooing was a cold business

Above right: 'Permafrost City'

Right: bears lower their heads when aggressive

44

downwind, and found her departure difficult to understand when suddenly the skidoos of Mike and Birger appeared round a bluff. They had been searching areas some 10 kilometres to the north, and failing to find anything had appeared at the worst possible moment. It was the cruellest bad luck, and with such unbelievable coincidences apparently stacked against us I lost heart, and for the first time in four difficult weeks started to believe we might not succeed in filming a bear with cubs after all.

However, 28 March was a new day, and by facing adversity comes triumph. After Rasmus and I had searched all the likely terrain on the coldest day so far, with the temperature −34°C, we headed along the sea ice to the most southerly tip of Edgeöya. Just as Rasmus was gazing out to sea past Negerpynten, dreaming perhaps of his homeland, my heart leapt with joy for there, on the most southerly snow bank on the island, was a polar bear den. A large plug of snow lay by the entrance, and fresh tracks led 30 metres down the slope, then back up to the den.

We shook each other's hands in delight, then remembering all the other disappointments, tempered our enthusiasm by thinking the worst. Surely a female would not have cubs in such a dangerous spot as this, close to the sea ice where numerous male bears would be hunting? No, it was more likely to be a temporary den, for bears do 'hole up' for two or three weeks, to rest or weather a storm.

However, we could not be sure, so built a snow shelter out on the sea ice, about 100 metres below the den. As we did so a head appeared, and watched us briefly, but there was no further activity. We pulled out at dusk, anxious to return as soon as there was enough light to travel.

We rose at 5 a.m. to a beautiful clear dawn. It was now −37°C and a bit chilly! As we reached the sea ice near the den, a mirage effect lifted the distant pack ice into the sky and these illusory towers rose and fell in the heat from the sun. We filmed this hypnotic Arctic rarity, then rushed towards the den, afraid of missing the female, in case she chose to leave on such a fine morning.

*Below left:
three-month-old
bear cub*

*Below: ice
crystals create
a double sun*

As we approached she did leave the den, walking down the hill before investigating our ice hide. She sniffed around, then climbed in the back way but rather inconsiderately re-emerged straight out through the front wall! Even more disturbing was the way she failed to return to the den but instead headed out into the pack ice, beyond the black rock point. It had been a temporary den after all, and now, used to these setbacks, we set off in pursuit in order to film her activity in the ice.

Our disappointment at yet another useless den changed to happiness as we filmed some really unusual scenes. A large male bear appeared in a mirage, and as he walked the frozen sea in search of seals, wobbled and shimmered in a desert of ice and creamy water. He passed our female who gave him a wide berth, then both drifted away into the haze.

Returning to our hide to inspect the damage, I suddenly became aware we were being watched, and looking up at the den, saw a bear's face blinking at us in the bright sun. It was a large female, so the other bear had been a visitor and we were still in business. We dived into the remains of our snow house but had to wait until mid-afternoon before her head appeared for just a few seconds. By then the sun had gone and the wind further chilled us. We had learnt to read the signs of hypothermia during our survival course: drifting concentration, uncharacteristic behaviour, shivering, stumbling, defects of vision and unconsciousness. Sitting still all day in an ice hide at −37°C had taken me to stage 3. If I stopped shivering I might be in trouble, so we rapidly motored home and I climbed into a sleeping bag with a hot drink. I was really cold, but within a couple of hours some warmth had returned to all except hands and feet, and I slept soundly.

Next day the female's head appeared just twice in ten hours of waiting, but at least she looked very relaxed and we still hoped she had cubs. Just in case we had got it wrong yet again, Mike and Birger continued searching other valleys for alternative dens.

31 March was once again cold, clear and crisp – a beautiful spring day, and just after we had settled in the hide, hundreds of guillemots started arriving on the nearby cliffs of Negerpynten. We marvelled at this clamorous spectacle, for this first sign of summer's profusion seemed incongruous on a day when the temperature was −31°C. However, seabirds must start early if they are to complete their breeding cycle before the snows return in September.

The nesting ledges were still covered with snow and ice, but the birds clung on and fought over the prime sites. So intense were these battles that the birds were often locked together, beak to beak, falling from the high cliffs until they hit the sea ice. An arctic fox was well aware of this event, for we filmed it waiting below, then rushing forward to grab a guillemot that was too engrossed in combat to notice. The fox buried the bird beside an iceberg and returned to the cliffs for more.

As if in response to the sun, the female bear appeared at 9.30 a.m. and immediately climbed out of the den. She yawned and stretched and her joy at release from four months entombed in an ice cave seemed very evident. She

46

slid down the mountain on her back, head wallowing in the powder snow, legs waving in the air. She rubbed her back to and fro, then rolled on to her front and rubbed her belly, eventually stopping her rapid descent by pushing her huge paws in front and snow-ploughing a deep furrow. She looked very thin, a sign perhaps that she did have cubs, but when she came down on to the sea ice and disappeared to the north until only a tiny speck, we really felt in more despair than ever before. Rasmus had never seen a mother travel more than a kilometre from a den with cubs, and our female was now four kilometres away.

We just sat and prayed and waited and, as if somebody up there loved us, the female did finally turn round and within three hours was back in the den. It had been a long three hours.

In the afternoon she popped out again, briefly, and there between her legs was a cub. We danced a discreet jig, shook hands, smiled, and screamed a silent shout of triumph. The sense of elation was intense, and though she didn't reappear again that day, we felt sure we would finally film our vital sequence. We told Mike and Birger the good news that evening, then watched a large male bear walk past the cabin in the twilight of an Arctic night – life felt wonderful again.

It was 1 April. What twists of fate would play their hand today we thought? Surely we cannot be sure of succeeding even now, but another wonderfully calm sunny day gave us a chance. The bear appeared at about 8.30 a.m., blinked briefly in the bright light, then climbed out and sat by the den entrance. A cub soon appeared, then another, and as she walked amongst them I felt sure I saw a third. Within moments it was confirmed; there were three cubs, a most unusual phenomenon, for one or two are more usual, though four have been recorded. So lady luck had at last turned in our favour.

The smallest cub was hardly the size of a rusty white terrier, whereas the other two were a more normal dumpy dog size, and quite white, certainly paler than their rather yellow-white mother. Their first sight of the outside world was greeted with terrified squeaks, and they looked down the steep mountainside with trepidation. The den was about 150 metres above the sea ice, and somehow they had to get down. The female fussed over them, then walked a few confident paces down, whilst two of the cubs followed gingerly, sliding backwards, with claws clutching the snow. The other stayed in the den entrance and cried so loudly that the female returned, and suckled all three in the sun.

They slept for an hour, then clambered up and down the slope, slowly growing in confidence, before returning to the den. I hoped they would be around for two or three days so we could film the cubs playing and suckling, but at 2 p.m. the female emerged purposefully, and started down towards the sea ice, followed protestingly by the little cubs. Perhaps she realised how vulnerable this spot was, for she had already been visited by two bears, and she must have watched others out on the ice. Or perhaps she was really hungry, for raising three cubs must have placed great demands on her reserves. Whatever the reason, her determined move out onto the ice was a last disappointment, but we followed discreetly, and interspersed with sleep and suckling, she was soon three kilometres from the shore and deep into the cover of the pack ice. Amongst the chaos of ice blocks she would probably be able to hide from marauding male bears, and she was now in the realm of the seal, and within sight of her first meal for four months. We bade them a fond farewell and watched their departure into a white haze, feeling very sad it was all over. Between us we had travelled 8000 kilometres to capture about ten minutes of edited film; that is about 500 kilometres sledging per minute, or eight kilometres per second. We hoped the audience would feel it was worthwhile.

As for us, we had seen the Arctic at its best, and its worst. It had been a tough but exhilarating trip. It was an adventure that few others could ever hope to experience and every moment, however cold, however difficult or depressing, now seemed worthwhile. It had been a rare privilege to share that remote island with the bears, and we knew how lucky we had been.

Mother and four-month-old cubs

48

THE SONG OF THE WALRUS

2 April 1984 was the date on which our mother polar bear and her three small, vulnerable cubs spent their first hazardous day roaming the jumbled sea ice south of Edgeöya. On that day exactly one year earlier, Hugh and myself were at the very start of a trip that was to take us to almost the same latitude north but nearly 3000 kilometres further west, to Dundas, one of the High Arctic islands of Canada. We hoped there to film the elaborate courtship displays of walrus, with the help of Ian Stirling, a scientist from the Canadian Wildlife Service, who is making a long-term study of Arctic marine mammals. We already knew how fortunate we were to have Ian Stirling as one of our scientific advisers. He has spent over twenty years researching Arctic and Antarctic marine biology and has become a leading authority on the subject. We looked forward to our first field trip in his company.

As with so many of our filming expeditions over the next two years, our operating base and point of contact was to be Resolute on Little Cornwallis Island. Ian was not due until 8 April, leaving us a useful period to film other vital sequences – aerials of the surrounding landscape, a herd of winter musk oxen if we could find one, and the activity around Resolute for our third film about man in the Arctic. Even though Resolute is the most northerly airport in Canada to which scheduled jet airliner services fly, even the Boeing 737s are divided half for freight and half for passengers, and rarely have an empty seat or cargo space left.

This is certainly not due to Resolute's setting. Little Cornwallis Island is a true Arctic 'desert' island, with low rounded hills, relatively few plants and land animals, and a reputation for collecting some of the worst weather conditions in the High Arctic. The attraction for all this coming and going from the south lies not in the scenery but because, from small beginnings as a temporary military supply camp, Resolute has now grown into a major base for the oil and mineral exploration industry, the Canadian communications

49

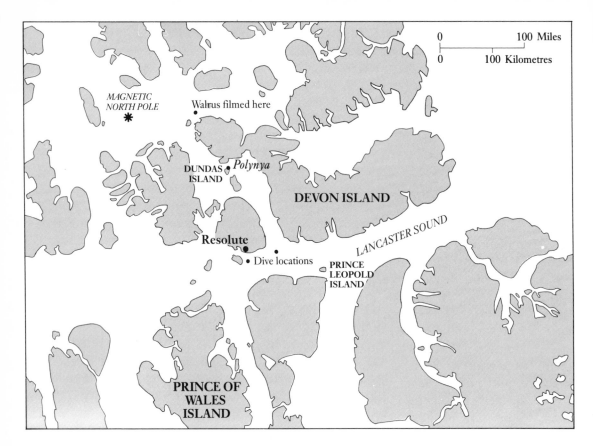

and weather service and, more importantly at least for us, the Polar Continental Shelf Project.

Polar Shelf, as it's affectionately known, is funded by the Canadian government and must have contributed more to basic research in the Arctic over the last fifteen to twenty years than any other single organisation. Between March and October, Polar Shelf maintains aircraft, helicopters, living accommodation, canteens, workshops, equipment supplies, storage sheds, fuel depots, and a radio communication system covering the entire Canadian Arctic.

We learnt very early in our research for the film series that, because of these facilities, virtually every notable scientist concerned with Arctic ecology would at one time or another pass through Resolute on the way to or from some remote research camp. Talking to them whenever possible would prove a better way to increase our understanding of the Arctic than any number of textbooks.

When we first wrote to Dr George Hobson, the director of Polar Shelf, asking if we could possibly stay at the Resolute base camp, charter their helicopters and generally take advantage of the set-up, his reply came as a timely warning that the reputation of film-makers was far from good. So many 'media people' bring with them an exaggerated self-importance and make such unreasonable demands that George's response was understandably guarded. During a phone conversation confirming our first visit to Resolute, he called us, half-jokingly, 'goddam photographers' – a title which amused us greatly and which we've used in correspondence with him ever since!

Under the circumstances, all the staff were helpful and welcoming, none more so than the overworked, slightly harassed base manager, Barry Hough. Barry certainly had enough problems coping with the usual flock of visiting scientists, plus 'Operation Cesar', a massive oceanographic research camp near the North Pole, without having to bother about us as well. In addition, two of his three available helicopters had recently crashed. Nevertheless, he found us a couple of beds in the hostel and promised he would do all he could to get us on to any interesting flights that had space.

It is excusable for a first-time visitor to imagine mistakenly that Resolute consists only of the airfield and its immediate surrounds. After all, the huddle of low snow-buried buildings provide every need, from the inevitable Hudson Bay store, a post office and a bar, to the various hostels including the one at Polar Shelf where we were staying. Organisations like Pan Arctic Oil, Dome Petroleum, Bradley Air, the Geological Survey of Canada, and many more, have workshops and storage sheds here, whilst stretching up the slope to the north is a vast area where thousands of barrels of fuel and piles of building materials and exploration equipment are stored, some of it never to be used. There is a continuous bustle of activity: planes and helicopters fly in and out, snow ploughs and trucks trundle around the airfield, and heavily-muffled people scuttle between one overheated haven and another. In the cold air, every exhaust pipe produces great plumes of vapour and the fume stacks on each building vigorously billow out clouds of steam. It is a reminder of the sheer volume of energy needed to keep a place like this running – energy in the form of oil and gas which, in the future, might well come from right here in the Arctic.

Five kilometres down the road on the curving shores of the bay lies a different, pleasanter Resolute – the Eskimo village: home to about 160 people, settled there in government-built houses during the 1950s. Before that date, many Inuit still lived a semi-nomadic life, moving from one area to another depending on the season of the year and the availability of animals that they could hunt for food. The people of some of the smaller, isolated settlements still lead a mainly hunting and trapping existence, even moving out to temporary camps for a few weeks in the spring and summer. In larger settlements, many people exist primarily on government welfare payments, and hunt only for the fun of it or to help keep traditional skills and values alive. Such places can be somewhat depressing to visit, caught as they are between the organised materialism of the white man's world without the employment and educational opportunities to properly supply it, and an ancient culture perfectly adapted to enable people to survive without too much difficulty in this harsh environment.

Resolute probably falls somewhere between the two extremes. Activity around the airfield base at least provides a number of well-paid regular jobs and some further seasonal employment – that is, so long as Canada can afford

Overleaf: dog teams are still used by polar Eskimos

its present level of spending on Arctic research and development, a question particularly relevant in today's more stringent economic climate. For the rest of the people, a handful of older men do still hunt seriously, trekking across the sea ice to find ringed seals or to shoot caribou on the nearby islands. And the settlement quota of thirty-eight polar bears is usually taken.

After two days of poor weather around the base, our first chance of a flight came on 4 April. Barry Hough told us that a fuel supply run was to be made south to Prince of Wales Island and that, with luck, our request to film musk oxen might be possible on the return journey.

Even the short time spent loading the camera equipment and other gear on to the aircraft made us realise that it was the coldest day we had yet experienced. The thermometer read −42°C and, although it was clear and bright, the brisk northerly wind made it seem even colder. A chart on the canteen notice board warned of the dangers of wind chill, and with the wind speed today an estimated 15–20 mph, the equivalent temperature could be as low as − 70°C. This was well within the 'exposed flesh may freeze in thirty seconds' bracket, so we would have to be careful filming outside.

Although there are a few ancient Dakotas (Douglas DC-3s) still flying, the De Havilland Twin Otter aircraft is now the Arctic's standard work-horse. A superbly rugged, adaptable design, it is capable of taking twenty-one passengers on fold-down seats or 1400 kilos of freight (the equivalent of eight 200-litre drums of fuel), or any combination of the two. The planes can land and take off in a ridiculously short length, using skis on ice and snow, or oversize balloon tyres for rough off-airstrip work in the summer. The remarkable handling and navigation feats of pilots who fly them in the usually difficult, sometimes appalling, conditions of the far north provide endless suppertime stories. None more so than the lanky grey-haired man, jacket flapping open as if it were a summer day down south, who nonchalantly walked across the snow that morning, swung himself into the pilot's seat, cast a quick experienced eye over the usual bank of dials, and began taxiing our aircraft for take-off.

Duncan Grant is one of those rare characters who become legends in their own lifetime. But we appreciated him as our pilot that day not just for his legendary flying skills but because of his consuming interest in Arctic history and wildlife. We had talked with him for several hours the previous evening and found that, because of his unusual habit of flying very low on most of his journeys, he knew better even than many biologists the whereabouts of musk oxen, caribou, wolves, whales and walrus throughout the High Arctic islands. He felt confident that he could land us near a herd of eighteen to twenty musk oxen that he had spotted a week ago while flying the same route as today. But first we must drop off the seven barrels of fuel.

As we flew south over the solid ice of Peal Sound, Duncan occasionally veered over to Somerset Island on the left or Prince of Wales on the right to point out small groups of Peary caribou or musk oxen, often in the exact positions he had predicted. He also drew our attention enthusiastically to several locations which were important in the history of Arctic exploration –

particularly the nineteenth-century British preoccupation with finding a way through the North West Passage, which led to Franklin's ill-fated voyage, with his ships *Erebus* and *Terror* and 129 officers and men, down this very strait in 1845, only to vanish thereafter from the known world.

The many expeditions sent to these regions after 1850 in the vain hope of finding Franklin and his men and for mapping the High Arctic islands are the subject of over twenty ship's journals and books of the time, all of which Duncan Grant has studied in great detail. With his immense knowledge of the area gained from thousands of hours of low-level flying, it wouldn't surprise me if some day it is he who solves for good the mystery of what really happened to Franklin. But if you ask him whether he already knows, he just gives a wily grin and says, 'Maybe, son – maybe!' – and changes the subject.

Having unloaded the drums of helicopter fuel on the south coast of Prince of Wales Island, we flew inland until Duncan located a group of eighteen musk oxen for us. Hearing the aircraft land, they ran off a short way to some high ground before turning to form their characteristic defence formation. Calves and yearlings are pushed to the centre of a semicircle of bulls and cows who stand, horns outward, facing the intruder – often a wolf, but in this case Hugh and myself creeping forward to try and get close enough to film.

The desolate landscape of gently rolling hills glazed by ice and snow made it difficult to imagine how these animals find enough to eat. Their range at these latitudes is covered by snow for eight months of the year, of which four months are in darkness, so most of the time they must paw through the surface crust to forage on the meagre lichens and remnant vegetation below. The cold, as now, can be extreme. Without their remarkable two-layered coats they would never survive.

The bearded one – 'Oomingmak' (as the Inuit call the musk ox) – is covered all over, except for the horns, hooves, lips and nose, with an under-layer of short fine wool of exceptional warmth. (This is the prized 'qiviut', which some think is superior in quality even to cashmere.) A much longer outer coat of shaggy, coarse hair up to 62 centimetres long covers the under-layer and hangs nearly to the ground, giving the musk ox its massive, prehistoric appearance. This impression is made complete by the extremely shaggy mane, especially noticeable on bulls, who have larger horns which merge at the base to form a massive, heavily ridged and furrowed boss, suitable for cushioning the impact of head-crashing fights during the autumn rut.

Even though we were dressed in many layers of high-quality expedition clothing, we shivered in the intensely cold wind and couldn't help admiring these superbly-adapted animals who cope with these conditions without any problem. It is never the cold as such that causes the deaths of musk oxen or caribou but, more particularly, a lack of food when rain or thawed snow freezes over the ground to form a hard and impenetrable sheet which can effectively lock away any suitable vegetation for weeks upon end.

We took some quite good shots of the musk oxen, although they never totally relaxed. Eventually they spooked and ran off to form another defence circle in the distance. We had only been out of the aircraft for half an hour, but standing face on to the cutting wind had been unpleasant, so that the decision not to follow them was easy. My right cheek and Hugh's nose and fingers had turned numb and white, but we recognised the signs of frostbite early enough and so avoided any permanent damage. Bob Barton, our Cairngorm instructor, would have been proud of this well-taught vigilance!

On the return journey to Resolute, and on two other flights during the next few days, we were able to film some very useful aerial scenic shots. With his mastery of the Twin Otter, Duncan was able to fly slowly and slightly crabwise, to give Hugh an excellent and steady camera-viewpoint out of the co-pilot's window. On one occasion he flew like this alongside the towering 300-metre cliffs of Prince Leopold Island and Devon Island where, later in the year, we planned to film some of the millions of seabirds that flock from the south to breed on them. At this time of year, in April, the nesting ledges were packed with snow and ice: inhospitable lines of dazzling white against the dark brown rock.

*Below: musk oxen
in a blizzard*

*Far right: large
male musk ox*

Ian Stirling arrived in Resolute on 7 April, and the next day set off north to Dundas Island in a helicopter, whilst we followed in Duncan's Twin Otter with the usual planeload of food, heating fuel, camera gear and scientific equipment. It was good to be heading for the 'field' again with the prospect of showing some aspects of walrus behaviour which, to the best of our knowledge, hadn't been filmed before. If we were lucky, a substantial number of these impressive animals would be living in the area of permanent open water that lies off the northern tip of Dundas. Having flown over several hundred kilometres of very solidly-frozen sea during the last few days, it was difficult to imagine *any* patch of water remaining clear of ice throughout the winter, but it does happen and the areas are known as polynyas.

A scientific paper recently written by Ian Stirling had given us the basic background to this unexpected phenomenon. 'Polynya simply means an area of water surrounded by ice. If it occurs in the same position every year, like the one at Dundas Island, it is known as a recurring polynya. In terms of biological significance it is these recurring polynyas that appear to be of critical importance to Arctic marine birds and mammals for feeding, reproduction and migration.

'Polynyas vary greatly in size and shape, the largest and most famous being the "North" water of Smith Sound and north-western Baffin Bay, which was first reported by William Baffin in 1616. Smaller, year-round polynyas are found in several areas of the Arctic where the sea ice is prevented from freezing over by the combined effects of tidal currents and wind, often magnified by shallow water or geographical constrictions.'

After a flight of only fifty minutes we spotted our polynya at the southern end of Penny Strait. It showed up clearly as a small, deep-blue patch of water against the brilliant white sea ice which stretched, otherwise unbroken, all around. We could also see the tiny green hut which was to be our home for the next few weeks, perched precariously on the edge of the high cliff bordering the polynya. Most of the snow had blown off the top of the island, leaving an impossibly rocky terrain, so Duncan landed on the sea ice about six kilometres south-east, and we chucked out all the gear and transferred it to sling nets ready for hooking underneath the chopper.

We carelessly allowed our survival gear (sleeping bags, rations and so on) to be winched away in the very first load, a stupid mistake, poignantly emphasised by a sudden deterioration in the weather. The freshening wind made us very cold and the scene rapidly became obscured by swirling ice crystals. We realised only too well how quickly we might perish in these conditions if the returning helicopter was unable to find us, and took it as a timely reminder to be more careful in the future. As it happened, the pilot did return safely, and flew us straight to the hut without picking up the other net. Visibility was deteriorating, and pilots are naturally wary of the great danger of flying in a sudden 'white-out': this is when most crashes occur.

The rest of the day was taken up with sorting stores and battling to erect the radio aerial against the biting gale. It was difficult to see much of the polynya now, but the few glimpses of walrus were encouraging. Although the water must have been very chilly, it steamed like a hot cauldron in the even colder air.

We were thankful that evening to get the stove lit, which, in a tiny three-metre by six-metre hut, warmed things up nicely. The wind set up a symphony of whistles through each tiny crack, and when the door was opened the inrush of cold air condensed into an impressive cloud of vapour. It made every exit and entry quite theatrical!

The following two days were virtually obscured by a continuous blizzard. We ventured out a few times for want of exercise, and on one occasion spotted a herd of fifteen walrus nearby. They looked completely at home in this wild-looking scene, gambolling amongst the loose ice at the edge of the polynya, protected from the cold by the thick layer of blubber which lies immediately below their grey, warty-looking skin.

This group was a mixed one – mothers with calves of various ages, some juvenile males and females, and a massive adult male which Ian guessed to be about three metres in length and to weigh perhaps 275 kilos. Its curved ivory tusks looked considerably longer than those of the females and would be impressive weapons against other males if need be. However, their tusks are more often used for hooking on to the ice as some were doing then, or possibly for stirring up the sea-bed in the search for shellfish.

In reality, the tusks are overgrown canine teeth, hanging down from the corners of the mouth through fleshy top lips, which themselves are covered by a wide moustache of tough, long bristles. Their heads look ridiculously small for the size of their large, ponderous bodies and no one could describe them as anything but ugly. Yet to watch them then was to appreciate the beauty of nature's adaptations: physical attributes which allow these extraordinary animals to thrive this far north throughout the year.

As we admired their antics down below, Ian told us that knowledge of walrus biology and behaviour was extremely scanty. Females are thought to breed first when between five and ten years old, and males to mature between six to eight years of age. Mating seems to take place from January to April, with the males displaying to the females in the water – the reason why we had timed our visit to Dundas then. The calves are born about fifteen months after fertilisation as, although gestation is only eleven months long, it's thought that a three- to five-month delayed implantation of the embryo into the uterus might occur, just as in other amphibious mammalian carnivores – or pinnipeds, as they are called.

For now, the wind made it impossible to film; but that sighting gave us great encouragement. Every trip was a gamble, but it looked as if we might get some good film if and when the weather improved. For the rest of the time there was plenty of chance to mend clothing, service camera equipment and natter at length with Ian about more general matters Arctic.

Although best known for his extensive polar bear work, Ian Stirling naturally extends his interest to the animals that bears prey on – like ringed seals and walruses. But he doesn't even stop there, because, like nearly all the other scientists that we have had the good fortune to work with during these

Lifting our gear off the sea ice

Far right: Dundas Island polynya

The land is glazed with ice

Far right: bears are good swimmers

last two years, he cares passionately about the future health of the Arctic as a whole. Now, with the violent wind buffeting our tiny hut, we poured ourselves another coffee from the freshly-made pot (it's known as a 'two-pot morning' when the weather is this bad), and Ian takes the chance to explain his work and thoughts in more detail.

'I've spent most of my working life in the polar regions, but I suppose because I'm a Canadian and have really enjoyed the Canadian Arctic I would like to feel I've made a certain contribution to this part of the world. More simply, I find that the biological questions about polar animals fascinate me in the same way as some people are captivated by deserts or coral reefs.'

Thoughts of hot sun and white sandy beaches crossed our minds, but the snow swirled on past the window and Ian continued, 'When you visit places like this you can see the environment right now just as it's been for hundreds of thousands of years, and that's a privilege that a person can't enjoy in many parts of the world any more. An enormous portion of Canada is taken up by Arctic regions and it's here that geologists have found vast reserves of oil, gas and minerals, which naturally people would like to exploit and use. At the same time, we have some marvellously rich areas, biologically speaking, so there's an obvious conflict between resource exploitation and conservation. But to be able to tell whether a proposed oil well or gold mine might be harmful to an area we need much more basic information about just how Arctic ecosystems work.

'My particular interest is the marine environment, firstly through helping to maintain large and healthy populations of polar bears, then in trying to understand how the ocean food chain operates – from tiny shrimps to the seals and so on that bears eat – and lastly to assess how important special places, like this polynya out here, really are to various sea mammals and to the Arctic Ocean's overall food production. With all the activity of oil and gas exploration and shipping – great icebreakers might be capable of smashing their way through to here in winters to come – we have to be concerned about wise conservation, wise use of areas to minimise the detrimental effects. It would be nice to think that after all the oil and gas has been taken out of a particular area, the place can revert back to the animals and we won't have damaged the habitat too severely in the process.'

Concluding with this thought, Ian suggested that we ventured out again in the ill-judged hope that the weather was improving. Hugh managed to take a few shots of ice and rime moving across the water surface to indicate the fierce currents that keep the polynya open, but the camera connections froze up after a while. A single walrus was right below the cliff at one time and Ian thought it was an adult male displaying. He wouldn't be sure until he could listen to its calls through an underwater microphone (or hydrophone, as it is known). His plan was to lower one of these hydrophones into the water, connecting it to a recorder in the hut through 300 metres or more of heavy-duty cable laid down the cliff. But it wasn't until Monday 11 April that the weather brightened up enough for us to get on with this vital task.

With improved visibility we could see the full extent of the polynya for the first time. The open water was about four kilometres across, set in a flat expanse of sea ice stretching to the mountains of the Grinnell Peninsula beyond: a very impressive and beautiful sight, with our hut probably the only human infringement in an otherwise empty landscape stretching to the North Pole.

We cut steps down a 100-metre snow gully to the ice edge below to find a position for the hydrophone. It was sunny and sheltered down there, and the scene amongst the stranded icebergs and on the flat shelf of ice by the water's edge was quite breathtaking. Three sets of polar bear prints reminded us to be on guard at all times. Hugh and myself went back up to the hut to start unreeling the long hydrophone cable down the cliff while Ian stayed below to retrieve the dangling end. The work proceeded well until a call on the radio from Polar Shelf made me rush inside. My diary continues the story: 'Took a message about the helicopter due to arrive later this afternoon and mistakenly thought Hugh was attending to the heavy reel, but he had in fact started down again to do some filming. When I came out of the hut and saw that the reel wasn't there any more I was horrified. It must have slipped off its mount and gone over the edge right above where Ian was standing. I knew that if it had struck him on the head it would probably have killed him, but couldn't see far enough over the edge to find out. Ran to the snow gully and glissaded down as quickly as possible, using the ice axe as a brake, overtaking Hugh on the way.'

With great relief we found Ian uninjured. Luckily he had felt the cable loosen and had looked up in time to see the whole thing hurtling towards him. Everything was now in a terrible muddle, and although we eventually managed to get the hydrophone into the water and connect it to the tape recorder in the hut above, a test revealed one or more breaks somewhere along the line, so the whole cable had to be laboriously reeled in again. We felt guilty that Ian's research plans had been put back by this accident, but thankful no one had been hurt.

Soon afterwards a helicopter arrived from Resolute bringing one of Ian's research colleagues, Wendy Calvert, to help with the walrus observations. Wendy is a member of Ian's group based in Edmonton and has worked with him for several years on the population and distribution of various Arctic marine mammals such as seals, and on the behaviour of polar bears and, more recently, these walruses here at Dundas Island. Ian decided to return with the helicopter to Resolute and bring out another hydrophone cable the following day, just in case we couldn't repair the damaged one.

As it happened, the scene next day was mostly obscured by blowing snow which also prevented Ian's return. We struggled in poor conditions to film no less than three polar bears which passed along the edge of the polynya during the day. One plunged into the water and swam into the distance amongst the floating ice, emphasising just how perfectly adapted these animals are to this seemingly hostile environment. When a male walrus began a display in view of the cabin, Wendy was able to explain the regular sequence of blowing and diving that takes place. Once the hydrophone was working we would be able to hear how the underwater sounds synchronised with the actions.

Far left: the sea freezes rapidly out of the current

Middle left: filming walrus at 77° North

Left: walrus singing

Below: walrus resting by Dundas

That night must have been extremely cold sleeping on the floor, for in the morning the sleeve of my sweater had frozen solid and I couldn't get it on! Wendy and Hugh thought it was amusing at least. We were all delighted, however, at a clearance in the weather. Ian arrived by 10 a.m. and by evening we had the new cable down the cliff and connected up without further problems. There was a large herd of walrus hauled out on the ice about a kilometre to the east, so we hoped they would come nearer tomorrow. Then in the silence of evening, with a red sun grazing the hills of Devon Island, we heard the powerful blow of a large male walrus in the water below, rippling the still reflection of sunset with his swimming display. It was too dark to film, so Ian turned on the hydrophone and at last we could listen to the 'song' of the walrus.

The sounds we heard were a total surprise: a series of distinct rhythmical drum beats, getting faster and faster before slowing down again towards a run of cymbal crashes and a final, unearthly gong. It was difficult to believe that an animal could make such a range of mechanical noises, and when two distant males started singing in opposition to our own soloist it sounded as if a Caribbean steel band was tuning up underwater! We listened for an hour or so, enchanted and amused, realising how evocative a sound track this would make to accompany whatever behaviour we might be able to film in the coming week or so.

The next two days were perfect – calm and sunny from breakfast to bedtime. The polynya looked beautiful in its various ways, changing mood with the tides, the floating ice and the direction of the sun. Only the occasional grunt of a distant mother walrus broke the immaculate silence. On several occasions, Hugh was able to get good shots of single males going through their elaborate display sequence, and now that the surface was still, we could also see the underwater part of the performance as they swam through the crystal-clear water, outlined against the stony bottom.

Sometimes a recognisable male displayed in roughly the same area for an hour or more, at other times for less, but each distinct song cycle took one and a half to two minutes and was repeated over and over again. Occasionally, while in the middle of his solo, another male would approach also in full voice. When this happened the tape recorder could hardly cope with the crescendo of noise. Then suddenly they would both stop, lying motionless on the sea-bed in eerie silence until one or other swam off leaving the winner (if that is indeed what he was) to start his song cycle once more.

Ian's belief is that these vocal 'water ballets' – for even a huge, blubbery old male is an elegant mover in the sea – are certainly displays to attract females for mating, but also possibly to lay claim to a certain area of the polynya and defend it against other males. As the walruses went through their routine, Ian or Wendy described the visible actions – head up; blow; head down; dive; stay on bottom; and so on – into a recorder which ran simultaneously with the one taping the underwater vocalisations picked up by the hydrophone. By analysing these tapes in the laboratory they are now certain that they can recognise individual animals. Developed further, it might be feasible to listen in to walrus songs, trace certain known animals and thus learn more about their movements and behaviour.

Sometimes the hydrophone picks up the ghostly underwater wails as bearded seals call to each other. Interestingly, Ian's team have found that bearded seals have a recognisable 'dialect', dependent upon which area of the Arctic they live in. This fact might also help in monitoring the effects of change or disturbance on each sub-population of seals.

Within a few days we had enough footage of male walrus displays and, although we thought this would already make a memorable sequence, we desperately wanted to film some family behaviour with numbers of animals interacting with each other. Unfortunately, the herd of twenty or so mothers and juveniles stayed tantalisingly out of range to the east and it was not until the end of a relatively action-free day on 16 April that our luck turned. After supper Ian decided to go down to the ice-edge to check the hydrophone, so I went with him to take some stills. Just as we were nearing the water we noticed a large group of walrus floating towards us along the edge of the ice from the west. It was a rare moment of sheer magic as they swam close by us, blowing and dipping against the sunset, and we both enjoyed the sensation of being so near to these magnificent beasts. I could see Hugh at the top of the cliff going into action with his camera as they floated towards his viewpoint, and knew that he would be getting some strong footage.

We found out, when we returned, that there had been some entertaining behaviour in the water, following which most of them had used their tusks to hook on to some thin ice within view of the hut, before going to sleep. Walruses are negatively buoyant; they cannot float without finning, so have to hold on in this way to stop themselves from sinking while they rest. The alternative is to haul right out on to thicker ice, but they seem able to do both.

Early in the morning on Sunday 17 April, Dennis Andriashek arrived from Resolute. He is another member of Ian's Polar Bear Project, who has probably handled and tagged more bears than anyone else in the Arctic. Like Ian, he has a delightful, dry sense of humour and together they liven up any situation. While Dennis stayed at the hut to help Wendy with the walrus recordings, Ian generously suggested that we go with him in the helicopter for a sound recording trip north up Penny Strait. We landed a couple of times so that Ian could drill a hole through the ice for a twenty-minute recording of the underwater sounds. By doing this in exactly the same locations each year he can count the calls and make an estimate of the numbers of walruses and seals in the area.

At 77° North we spotted a large group of walrus hauled up on the ice near to a breathing hole. Ian landed us a kilometre away with the camera, guns and survival gear, and continued north with the promise to pick us up about two hours later. He also took the wise precaution of radioing our position to Barry at Polar Shelf just in case the helicopter couldn't make it back for some reason. Certainly, as the engine noise faded into the distance, we had the memorable feeling of being very remote from any other humans. We learnt later that the following year, on the sea ice very near to this spot, David Hempleman-

Adams, the young British explorer trying to reach the magnetic North Pole a further 160 kilometres north-west, had unfortunately had to kill an attacking polar bear. Happily, we had no such problem.

We stalked to within 20 metres of the walrus, using a jumbled area of small bergs for cover. The stench was almost overpowering, for by the look of it they had been defecating in the same area all winter. Nevertheless, they did look good on this marvellous clear day and we got some valuable shots as they scratched the hoar-frost from their bodies with surprisingly gentle flippers, and occasionally turned over in a great heap of pinkish blubbery flesh, long ivory tusks glinting in the sun.

That night, Ian and Dennis returned to Resolute to do some bear tagging around Devon Island, leaving Wendy and ourselves to continue recording walrus sounds and film anything else that might happen. We teased her relentlessly about many things, including the great honour of being here in this remote spot with two honourable (albeit middle-aged) English gentlemen to look after her! But she always seemed to manage the final riposte during this light-hearted banter. Anyway, we vowed to do most of the camp chores over the next few days to avoid any possible charge of male chauvinist piggery!

As it turned out, we had reasonable weather at Dundas on the next three days, whereas at Resolute it was unflyable all the time, preventing Ian from returning. The walruses virtually gave up on us and, apart from a few brief shots, were generally too far away to film. The polynya was enlarging rapidly now in the slightly warmer temperatures, and great sheets of ice, broken off from the edges, drifted across the open water. One morning we heard the first snow bunting call, a real herald of spring, and a raven croaked by overhead. We began to spend a lot of time talking about travel arrangements, wives, kids, holidays, hot sun on herbaceous borders and cricket! We had been in Canada for nearly two months altogether and longed to get home for a short break now that not much more could be achieved here in the way of film.

Our last day, Thursday 21 April, was one of sheer Arctic perfection. The thermometer read −20°C, which felt warm after the −40s we had become used to. There was only a faint breeze and miles of visibility. After filming some sequences with Ian for our third film about man's involvement in the Arctic, we bade him farewell and flew off in the early afternoon from a sparkling Dundas Island that had given us mixed fortunes over the last two weeks but, we hoped, some memorable images. Ian had brought letters from Sue and Vyv (our wives) which we read avidly on the flight to Resolute. By Tuesday 26 April we were back in England, but minus our film rushes, which had been mislaid in the far north. Luckily, someone discovered them in a shed at Cambridge Bay, an Inuit settlement on Victoria Island! It was a great relief when they eventually found their way back to London for processing a fortnight later and we knew for certain that all our efforts over the past weeks hadn't been in vain.

UNDER THE POLAR ICE

On 8 May 1984 we were once more in Resolute. Although a year later, this new visit to Canada started in effect about three weeks after returning from the marvellous Svalbard expedition. From now until the end of 1984, Hugh and I would split forces in order to have every chance of covering the frenetic burst of plant and animal activity so characteristic of the short Arctic summer.

Hugh was to be in East Greenland from early June to the end of July, while I journeyed around the Canadian Arctic with Martin Saunders, a BBC staff cameraman from Bristol who has built a reputation for himself, through his work on the BBC series *Life on Earth* and *The Living Planet*, as one of the world's finest wildlife photographers. He is well known also for relishing the more demanding and risky projects. On that criterion at least I felt sure that the next few weeks were not going to bring him disappointment. Both of us are qualified divers, and with Martin also an accomplished underwater camera-man, our plan was to film whatever lived underneath the sea ice during an Arctic spring. But first there was a mountain of gear to sort out at Polar Shelf, and contact to be made with Dr 'Buster' Welch, who had generously offered to help us achieve this objective.

Buster is a leading marine biologist with the Canadian Government's Department of Fisheries and Oceans. It was our good fortune that in May 1984 he was at the very start of a three-year research programme, aimed at finding out more about the natural productivity of the Arctic seas. The project involved an intensive programme of work underneath the sea ice before the July break-up. For this purpose he had moved his team into a self-contained range of buildings down on the shoreline of Resolute Bay, where an impressive range of equipment, including ice hole cutters, specialised transports, com-pressors and diving gear, had been assembled.

All Buster's colleagues generously agreed to give up as much of their valuable research time over the next couple of weeks as would be necessary to help us film the complex under-ice food chain. We had never thought that these sequences were going to be easy, but at least we had the best possible diving team to help us. Buster suggested that we make a trial dive without cameras the next afternoon, so we went to our beds in contemplative mood.

Kitting up, at base, for the dive the following day provided one of the funniest sights so far on this project – Martin Saunders being manhandled into a special diving suit a shade on the tight side. Already resembling a circus clown in his white thermal jump suit, he had to hold his arms above his head before being literally bounced through the narrow rubber neck ring like an awkward bundle being forced into an undersize sack. By the end of all this he was so red in the face and hot that I think he genuinely looked forward to getting out on to the ice!

I was also dressed in a beautifully warm and bulky 'woolly bear' suit, but had the simpler task of getting into a standard 'dry' suit, which although necessarily tight round ankles, wrists and neck, to keep out the water, at least had a zip across the back for ease of entry.

The dive-hole for that afternoon was five kilometres out on to the ice in Resolute Bay – about an hour's trip in their incredibly noisy Canadair Flex-track machine. This strange-looking track-propelled vehicle has been adapted by Buster's team into a very practical dive-support unit, complete with extra large-capacity compressed-air cylinders, two-way radio, heater and various pieces of water-sampling equipment for the scientific work. While resembling a cross between a tank and a toolshed as it trundles laboriously over the ice, it does enable everyone to get to and from a dive in comparative comfort and warmth.

We stopped by some flags marking a large sheet of plywood that lay on the ice. Pulling this to one side revealed today's dive-hole: a rectangle of clear, dark water, measuring about two metres by one metre. There was something incongruous about it – a tiny, ice-flecked swimming pool set in an endless frozen landscape. It would be wrong to pretend that either of us felt much enthusiasm for jumping into it right then, but we couldn't think of a suitable excuse to avoid the inevitable!

Martin had to go through more contortions to get the diving helmet fitted over his head and secured to the neck ring. Unlike the conventional scuba system where a compressed-air cylinder is taken down with the diver, Martin's fresh air would be fed to him through one rubber hose and his exhaust brought back to the surface through another. In this way, the bubbles that would normally be expelled underwater are avoided: less noise, less disturbance to the delicate life-forms under the ice ceiling, and certainly an advantage for photography. The umbilical connecting the dive suit to the Flex-track was completed by a safety line and a communications circuit which would allow Martin to talk to the team on the surface. For the moment, though, he seemed unusually silent as he poised himself to jump into the hole.

Eventually he took the plunge, but it was a while before he got used to the controls. Valves on the suit let air in and out to allow him either to sink or rise as needed. He would get a few feet underwater amongst a confusion of exhaust bubbles and then suddenly pop up to the surface with the suit inflated like a balloon! Bobbing around like this amongst the small chunks of floating ice was hardly an elegant start, but after a few more tries he did get the hang of it and sank smoothly down into the hole until he disappeared below the underside of the ice.

After a couple of minutes I called him on the intercom, anxious for a reaction. 'What's it like, Martin?' There was a pause and some heavy breathing. 'Bloody hell, Mike!' came the muffled answer, and then another silence during which I supposed he was looking round. 'Bloody amazing down here,' he added. His tone was even more descriptive than his words, and made me hurry to finish kitting up so that I could go down and see for myself. As the ice here was just over two metres thick, the first part of the dive was like swimming down a narrow tunnel. It would be dishonest not to admit to a slight feeling of apprehension on pushing underneath the ice for the first time. The safety line back up to the surface was reassuring though, particularly as an unexpectedly strong current tends to pull you away from the edge of the hole.

It took a moment to adjust to the comparative gloom before being able fully to appreciate Martin's initial reaction of amazement. The water was so incredibly clear that the underside of the ice – the 'ceiling' in effect – could easily be seen stretching into the distance. The amount of light reaching the water through the thickness of the ice was further reduced by a thin layer of greenish-brown algae growing on the under-surface of the 'ceiling'. There were places with less algae or thinner snow above, where the blue-tinged light could shine through more strongly, although still with a subtle effect.

Grazing upside down on the lush pasture of marine algae or swimming inverted in the water were millions of shrimp-like amphipods, while countless numbers of comb jellies in a variety of sizes and designs, some trailing long tentacles, drifted slowly by in the current. These ctenophores are all edged with lines of tiny, hair-like cilia, which beat in rhythmic patterns and presumably give the animal some control over depth and direction. If the light caught these cilia at just the right angle, an exquisite spectrum of colour sparkled brilliantly with each pulse of movement. Several species of jellyfish also drifted by – one with a very large light-blue body and orange tentacles being particularly beautiful. There was the occasional silvery flash from a polar cod – a fish about the size of a small trout and specially adapted to live permanently in these cold waters and feed on the abundant amphipods.

Where the sun shone down into the open sea through the dive-hole, it formed shafts of light, as if there were dust in the water. Looked at more closely, this 'dust' showed up as myriads of tiny, translucent animals called copepods, only just large enough to make out. It was a subtle climax to round off a spectacle of immense productivity, such a sharp contrast to the frozen 'desert' above the ice. No wonder biologists like Buster Welch and Ian Stirling are so keen to study the riches of these Arctic waters and care so fervently about their future health and conservation. Whilst the plants and animals on the surface are still locked into winter, down there, under the protection of a two-metre layer of ice, reproduction is already well under way to create a food

The dive-hole

*Below: taking
the plunge and
filming under
the ice*

Comb jelly

*Below: harp seal
under the ice*

Stranded iceberg

Below: bear checks on seal breathing holes

Below right: mother and one-year-old cubs

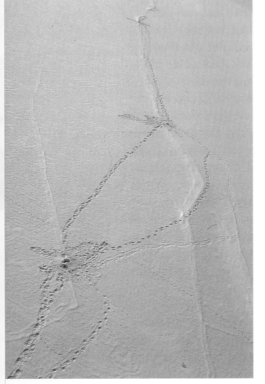

against the lighter patches of gravel, was a ringed seal slowly swimming forwards, looking up all the time. It must have been inquisitive, wondering perhaps who the strange invaders were, for it started to swim upwards heading directly towards Martin's camera, which fortunately he had left running on a slow-motion setting.

This graceful seal, its lovely ringed skin pattern now showing up perfectly, came to within a metre of the camera lens, paused for five or six seconds to take in the scene through a pair of large jet-black eyes and then, with the same leisurely movements as before, turned and swam slowly away into the distance. Chance occurrences like that often provide the high points, the real 'nuggets', of a film, and we hoped that we might get another chance to encounter ringed seals underwater before we left. Apart from their natural appeal, they play an important role very near to the top of the Arctic marine food chain. They are the main prey of polar bear so if ringed seal numbers fell, there would surely be an equal decline in the polar bear population.

For some reason, the coldest dive of our stay was also the most straightforward. The scientists had cut a hole 200 metres or so from the shore of the bay so that we could film in water shallow enough to be able to show the sea floor and the ice ceiling in the same shot. We also wanted to record the many clams and other shellfish which were living on the bottom in great numbers and which form the staple diet of walrus.

It's as well that there is such a profusion of shellfish, considering an adult walrus needs as much as 45 kilos of food per day. This would amount to 1000

Polar bear sniffing for seals

or more clams, of which only the soft feet or siphons are torn off to eat. It is likely that even when these shellfish are partially buried in the bottom sediment or hidden from sight by the darkness of winter, walruses can still find them by feeling around with the touch-sensitive bristles which cover their thick fleshy muzzles. It was believed that they used their tusks to dig out shellfish from the mud, but recent evidence suggests only the bristles are used.

In order to get enough footage in one session to illustrate walrus food as well as the range of other bottom-dwelling animals – from bright orange starfish and large sea squirts to small goby fish and squat lobsters – we stayed underwater for a total of two and a half hours, with only one ten-minute break to renew the air bottles. By the end of this time both Martin and myself were so cold that we had lost all feeling in our hands, feet and faces, and were most relieved to get back to base, where it took an hour or so to regain our circulation.

Little by little the under-ice footage was building up into a worthwhile sequence, so that at the end of two weeks we were pleased with our progress. When the weather was too bad to get out to one of the dive-holes, we filmed some of the smaller creatures like copepods and amphipods, using tiny acrylic tanks in the laboratory. All these animals were so sensitive to temperature that the water in their tanks had to be kept very cold to prevent them from quickly dying. During many conversations with Buster and the others we soon realised how little is yet known about the Arctic Ocean and why projects like theirs are so important. It is vital to gather basic biological information against which any changes that might occur in the future, through possible pollution and disturbance from oil, gas and mining operations, or all-season shipping, can be judged.

Buster Welch echoes many marine biologists when he calls the polar oceans 'the last great unexplored ecosystem'. As he pointed out, 'We only know in very sketchy fashion who eats what at certain times of the year from analysing stomach samples of animals like seals, whales and murres which have been killed by Inuit hunters. What we don't know is the flow of energy between the various plants and animals in the food chain, and just how much life the productivity of the Arctic seas could sustain. It's a bit like a farmer wanting to know how many cows he could raise on an acre without having any idea of the quantity of grass it produced. We know that there may be, say, 20,000 narwhals in the Arctic, but not whether the food base could in fact support 100,000. So this is the sort of information that is badly needed, although through ours and other work we are sure that the sea around Resolute and in certain other places in the High Arctic like Lancaster Sound is as productive as well-known fishing areas like Halifax much farther south.'

On a pleasantly sunny afternoon we filmed some of the operations that Buster's team have devised as ways of measuring this amazing productivity. The dive-holes in the ice were not cut with great labour merely for the benefit of us film-makers, but for the more serious purpose of taking samples from under the ice. So we filmed one of the scientists going down in the hard-hat diving suit dragging a hose connected to a vacuum unit inside the Flex-track.

At set intervals, he would suck off all the algae and any associated grazers from within an acrylic ring to be collected on the surface and later analysed in the lab. Light readings above and below the ice were taken simultaneously, and the thickness of the snow cover also measured. In this way, a picture can be gradually built up of the growth rate of the algae under various conditions and the numbers of animals that consequently feed upon it.

Film of elaborate and expensive work like this would be very useful for our third film. It would show the sort of lengths which scientists in the Arctic must go to in order to find out even such basic information. But there are always more ways than one to tackle a problem, as we found out when we filmed with Glen Cota, another marine biologist working out of Resolute.

Each season, Glen erects a laboratory about five kilometres out on the ice, using one of the bright orange 'Parcols' – a type of fully-insulated, temporary building in the shape of a Nissen hut, especially designed for Arctic camps. Inside the Parcol, Glen cuts a dive-hole, and around this lays a wooden floor. He then moves in a stove, boxes full of scientific instruments and laboratory equipment, bench tops, microscopes, lighting, comfortable chairs, books, a small computer and a microwave oven for cooking snacks! Outside, a generator is installed and kept running permanently. In this way Glen can settle down for long periods on the ice in comparative comfort while collecting water samples from his private ice pool. Although his work is aimed at finding answers to similar questions about productivity as Buster's, it isn't based on diving. Glen would find it difficult to get at the algal layer and its grazers, so he is more concerned with the plankton (the floating life-forms) that he can pull up easily in his water samples.

The attractions of this elaborate set-up for Martin and myself were twofold. First, we could film specimens of collected plankton under the high-definition microscope, and second, a young ringed seal had adopted Glen's sampling hole as a convenient alternative breathing place for itself and had become quite tame. Glen and his colleagues had nicknamed the seal 'Sea Biscuit', and with him we felt we had a good chance of obtaining some more underwater shots.

On several evenings, after Glen had finished his work and returned to Resolute, we skidooed out to the Parcol and sat in wait for 'Sea Biscuit'. Martin had considered trying to dive down the hole with him, but the current was generally too strong, so we settled for immersing the camera at the edge of the hole to get shots as he came up for breath and swam away again. We would be chatting quietly or reading maybe for an hour or so, when a noisy exhalation of breath would sound from the corner of the Parcol: 'Sea Biscuit' had arrived and would then be quite pleased to get some attention. Glen had warned us that the seal objected to anything left in 'his' water and certainly on the first occasion that 'Sea Biscuit' found a film camera and lights there he splashed them furiously with his front flipper! Initially perhaps he saw our paraphernalia as a threat, but after a few visits he seemed to get used to it and to us, and Martin was able to get a number of extremely useful and charming shots. It seemed extraordinary that a totally wild animal would, by the third evening, allow us to hold his flipper and would also close his eyes for his head to be stroked.

By 21 May we had amassed a useful amount of film material and felt it was definitely time to leave Resolute and allow research to assume its proper priority. Buster, however, thought that our imminent departure made a good excuse to organise an enjoyable group outing which could be combined with cutting a new dive-hole at a refrozen lead on the sea ice at the south end of Wellington Strait, some 45 kilometres east of Resolute. On a previous visit he had noticed an abundance of ringed seal breathing holes in the area. This was the sort of occasion when Buster Welch was at his most exuberant. Always enthusiastic, energetic and – I'm sure he would admit himself – far from quiet, he now went into overdrive as we prepared the sledges for the journey.

Perhaps because of having to cope safely with extreme conditions, scientists who work in the Arctic tend to be very practical, and Buster is no exception. A skilled worker in metal or wood, he had made both the beautiful four-metre-long sledges, or komatiks as they are called locally, out of banded strips of wood to a traditional Inuit design – very strong, yet flexible. Buster and his wife Cathy have gathered a host of such ideas from the local Inuit, many of whom they now count as amongst their closest friends. Indeed, having often lived all year round in various settlements, they have grown to love the Arctic and its people and appreciate the natural Inuk ability for ingenious craftsmanship. Cathy, for instance, has learnt how to make skin clothing – parkas and baggy trousers of caribou fur, worn together with completely waterproof boots made from the skin of the bearded seal.

Directly I showed enthusiasm for one of these superbly practical suits I was told by Buster to 'go get it on and see what it's like being dressed as an Inuk for a day'. I needed no more persuading and as we sped over the ice on that superbly clear but very cold day I felt more comfortable and warm than I ever had before, despite the expense of our European-style protective clothing.

The expected ringed seals unfortunately disappeared like shadows as soon as Martin went down the freshly-cut dive-hole, even though everyone spread out, like Inuit sealhunters, to cover all the other obvious breathing holes in a vain attempt to persuade the seals to use the new one near to the camera. However, Martin was enthusiastic about the underwater scenery at this spot, saying that the great dome of thinner ice where the open water lead had refrozen looked like a vast, subtly-lit cathedral roof. Work completed, we all enjoyed a few hours relaxing in that impressive landscape of tortured ice. In the shelter of a small berg we feasted on a slow-cooked arctic char, a type of northern sea-trout with a taste which must be the equal of the most expensive salmon. Then, while the others went off to get nearer to a passing polar bear, I lay down on the snow, impervious to the cold in my magnificent borrowed furs, and reflected on what a remarkable privilege we had been given over the last three weeks. We had, after all, with such generous help, been able to observe and film the sort of extraordinary scenes and creatures under the Arctic ice that very few people would ever get the chance to see.

BORN TO THE BARREN LANDS

Towards the end of May the Arctic begins to change dramatically. There have been twenty-four hours of daylight for a month, and the sun is now high enough and hot enough to start melting the snow. Life under the sea ice has begun to stir, walruses have displayed, polar bears have led their cubs out onto the frozen ocean, and during all this time the caribou have been trudging across hundreds of kilometres of Canadian tundra to reach their calving grounds.

My plan was to be there when the caribou arrived so, leaving Mike in England, I reached Yellowknife on 27 May to find that life does not always go to plan. Two vital boxes of equipment had been mislaid somewhere in Canada, the helicopter was still 1000 kilometres too far north, its fuel still not delivered to the campsite, the snow melt late and the caribou in the wrong place – it was not an auspicious start. Every filming trip is a combination of planning, logistics and optimism, yet it seemed that on this one we had only optimism left! However, one by one the problems were resolved; firstly the lost luggage.

I had flown to Yellowknife via Toronto and Winnipeg so the boxes must be at one of those places. They emerged in Edmonton! Once found they had to reach me by Sunday lunchtime for it was then that the next leg of the journey was due to take place. They made it with one hour to spare.

The helicopter was essential to the operation, for the Beverley Herd calving grounds are extensive, stretching across 200 square kilometres of treeless tundra either north or south of Beverley Lake. We did not yet know which area the caribou would choose, and even with a helicopter, we might have difficulty finding them. The machine had been due to fly down from Resolute the previous week, but some mechanical problem had caused a delay. The DC-3 that was to fly in with the helicopter fuel also had mechanical problems – it had crashed! The damaged undercarriage had to be repaired before we would be operational.

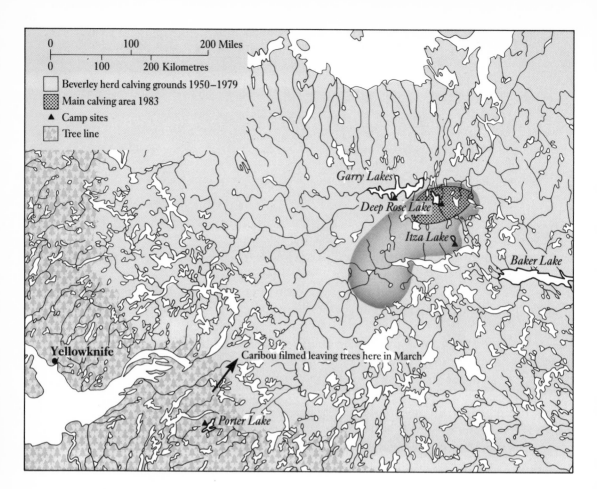

Just to add to these snags the thaw, or 'break-up' as the Canadians call it, was some two to three weeks late, thus delaying the caribou on their migration north. However, they are so adept at making up lost time that we felt sure the five main calving days around 9 June would not be seriously affected. Seemingly regardless of the weather, this period of peak activity varies little from year to year, for the rhythm of the Arctic seasons is as deeply etched in the caribou's memory as are the places where they themselves started life.

The more immediate effect of the late season were the lingering fog banks, caused by the rapid warming of the cold land and the extensive evaporation that takes place. We were now being baulked by one of these, ruining our intention of landing the Twin Otter and equipment on the frozen Itza Lake, close to the campsite. We had already flown 800 kilometres north-east of Yellowknife, and were frustrated to be held up just 10 kilometres short of our destination. But we had no choice and diverted south-east to the Inuit settlement of Baker Lake, another hour's flying.

Twelve hours later we made a smooth landing alongside the campsite. It was 30 May and spring really seemed to have arrived. The wind was calm, the sun warm, snow buntings sang and a patchwork of thawing hills and melting lakes stretched on all sides to far horizons – it was a wonderful wild spot.

82

Though I had travelled alone from England, I was accompanied from Yellowknife by Anne Gunn. I had previously met her at Porter Lake in March, when she and Frank Miller were counting caribou for a government census of the Beverley Herd. Frank was here to greet us, and with him was Eric Broughton, a government veterinary surgeon.

They had gathered at Itza Lake to continue a three-year study into the mortality of caribou calves, and the base camp at which we unloaded was some 50 kilometres south of the Beverley Herd calving grounds, the same caribou that we had filmed leaving the trees at the end of March. Having counted the herd, Frank and Anne now wished to find out how many calves survive to swell the ranks. Their report on the first two years' findings explains why.

'Migratory Barren-Ground caribou of the Beverley Herd are a primary source of fresh meat for several thousand native peoples, namely the Inuit, Dene and Métis. The Beverley Herd has, however, declined about 50% in size during the 1970s and that trend is likely to continue over the long run if rates of harvest increase, especially if animal kills approach the 1978–9 level. Increasing native populations, the use of modern hunting technology, and greater accessibility to the caribou makes it likely that future rates of harvest of the Beverley Herd will be at unsustainable high rates over the long term. Thus, intensive management of the herd will be necessary to maintain it for future generations to use.

'Although the caribou resource currently cannot be managed on a biological basis because of socio-political reasons that go far beyond the realm of renewable resource management, we continue to gather biologically sound information in the hope that it will someday be properly used. Therefore, we investigated the causes of mortality of newborn caribou calves to evaluate the importance of predation during the calving and early postcalving periods. If the people concerned with the management of the caribou and the primary users of the caribou eventually accept the need for conservation of caribou, we will be better able to provide good biological advice through our studies.'

As the situation outlined above applies to a greater or lesser extent to all the other caribou herds on the North American continent, and to some extent to other Arctic wildlife, it might be helpful if I enlarge on a few points mentioned in the report.

Firstly, the decline in herd size. Frank admits that it is notoriously difficult to count caribou, as the land in which they live is so vast. The herds tend to split up in the winter, so even if the main concentration is found and counted, you can never be sure that several thousand do not remain undiscovered somewhere out in the Barrens. There is also a credibility gap between the biologists and native people. The latter believe their estimates (they don't carry out aerial surveys) are more accurate. They also believe they are natural conservationists, having hunted caribou for centuries without wiping them out. However, they won't admit how many they now kill, neither do they appear to take into account their own rapidly rising population. There seems no doubt that the numbers of caribou are indeed falling.

Tundra polygons

Far left: the
spring thaw

It strikes us detached foreigners as a sad state of affairs, for both Inuit and biologist are working for the same purpose; both want the caribou herds to survive and flourish. But the Inuit don't want, and reckon they don't need, biologists, perhaps because they feel they are agents of a government they don't really trust. Though the Canadian government pours admirably large sums of money into research to ensure the herds survive, many Inuit still seem suspicious of their motives.

The fact is, apart from aesthetic considerations, each caribou is a very valuable animal and a healthy herd is indeed a renewable resource. If managed properly they can provide fresh meat for as long into the future as they have in the past. Each caribou provides about 45 kilos of meat and estimates made in 1983, taking into account the cost of transporting beef to the remote communities, calculated that each animal was worth about $500. Their value may be higher each year.

In the past, a family living on the land needed to kill between 200 and 300 caribou a year. This might seem a large number, but virtually every bit of the animal was used, providing food, fuel, clothing and skins for tents. Now the situation is different, for the government has encouraged native people to settle in communities and provided them with houses, heating, schools, in fact all the trappings of Western civilisation. Very admirable, but the Inuits' *culture* has not changed and they still want, indeed need, to hunt, so ingrained is the habit. And this is where the threat posed by modern hunting technology is felt.

In the past, an individual would go out alone with a sledge, dog team and spears. They now have motorised sledges, high-powered rifles, and worse still, two-way radios, so when someone finds the herd all the other hunters are able to move in for the kill. The Canadian government, seeming to contradict their concern for conserving the herds, encourages native peoples to return to the land (to reduce the cost of their subsistence policy) and provides aircraft to fly teams of hunters to the herds. In 1982–3 $22,000 was paid out for this purpose, and for all assisted hunting programmes a total of $1.3 million was spent.

The effect of all this technology is that often more caribou are killed than need be, and sometimes only the choicest cuts are taken home for the deep freeze. So the Inuit, who once lived in harmony with the wilderness, whose culture was one of the most astonishing examples of adaptation in the history of man, are now caught in the press of change, the twentieth century thrust upon them in a matter of just a few decades. As the famous Arctic traveller Fred Bruemmer said, 'Into his lifetime has been compressed 150 centuries of our own technological evolution.' The caribou are not the only casualties.

The government, rightly concerned at events in the north, have pursued a policy of pouring money into the area. I met a member of the Department of Economic Development, who explained his personal attitude to this policy. 'Spending money is not the answer. If the north's budget was cut back to the same extent as the southern territories of Canada, the people would die.' He added, 'It is the Third World we are dealing with. Communication is difficult –

difficult for us to get across what we require of them, and difficult for them to communicate their emotions and requirements to us.' He also pointed out, 'They are greedy, they want it all; support from the government, independence, rights to the land, a share in the mineral rights – and control of the wildlife resource.'

This is an attitude we heard expressed on a number of occasions, but the Inuit believe it is their land and of course they have a point. After all, they have lived there for centuries, and Western culture has not necessarily been accepted by choice, but thrust upon them by a Government that is trying to make native people conform to its attitudes and policies. Many Inuit regret the turn of events, the loss of their culture, the breakdown of social discipline, the lack of respect of the young for the old. This, they say, is why caribou are wasted – the modern hunter lacks the innate judgement of those who have had to live and survive on the land. However, they believe the caribou belong to them, and resent any intrusion from governments or biologists. And this is why the idea of caribou management is such a difficult political issue.

So the huge caribou herds that once roamed the Barrens are caught in the pressures of social change, and are threatened with extinction. Frank, Anne and Eric are trying to find out everything they can about the herds, so that if management is eventually decided on, everybody will have the necessary facts. Using the helicopter, their plan was to search the calving grounds for dead caribou, and as a percentage of cows and recently born calves die each year, it was important that they located the majority of the herd. Once found, they would search the peripheries of these concentrations, and when they moved on, search the areas themselves. Thus they would find the maximum number of dead caribou calves and cows with the minimum of disturbance to the herd. Each corpse would then be autopsied to try to establish the cause of death.

Within a day of our arrival, the DC-3 brought in the helicopter fuel, and two days later the helicopter itself arrived. We had been growing anxious about the loss of time, for none of us had any idea whether the caribou had arrived, and if they had, in which part of the calving grounds they would be. A couple of planes had reported seeing caribou to the south-west of our camp, and on the last day of May the first appeared on the southern horizon, dancing in the haze of the evaporating snow. So they were on their way, and with them came the spring, for the ground began to appear from beneath the melting snow and the scene took on an intricate pattern of black and white.

On 3 June, Frank and Anne went on their first recce north and by late evening we knew we were all in business, for the caribou had arrived in the heart of their calving grounds. They had also seen a wolf and a herd of twenty-four musk oxen with four very young calves. I was keen to film musk oxen whilst there was still snow on the ground, and a herd with two- to three-week-old calves would be particularly interesting, so we laid plans.

To save flying time and expense, I was to be taken north with camping gear and seven days' rations, dropped near the musk ox herd and then, after a day or two, moved to the heart of the caribou calving grounds, where I would camp alone for several days and try to film a birth. All this depended

Caribou calf

Far left: caribou mother attending to newly born calf

Below: shedding the afterbirth

every caribou herd chooses a calving ground where wolves are less likely to be present – that is why they travel so far north – the principal threat to calves during the two years of research was wolves. As Frank Miller sums it up, 'At present, wolves remain the most manageable of mortality factors in the life equation of caribou. We cannot emphasise enough, however, that killing wolves will be of no avail in the long term if human utilisation of caribou herds cannot be regulated. Demands for caribou in excess of the maximum level that the herd can annually replace through births will lead to the destruction of herds, regardless of the intensity of application of biologically sound management practices. Only enlightened users can save the large herds of migratory Barren-Ground caribou in Canada.'

In recent years, the most optimistic sign that these users will become enlightened is the formation of the Caribou Management Board. This is run by the Inuit themselves, with representatives sent from each settlement that hunts caribou. Also present are government representatives and biologists, and the frank exchange of views can only enhance the likelihood that the huge herds of caribou will continue to roam the Barrens for many years to come.

Arctic fox moulting

SUMMER OF THE MIDNIGHT SUN

'This really is one of the most beautiful places in the world, the sea still frozen, the land covered with pristine snow crystals, the horizon punctuated by dramatic peaks that tower into a clear blue sky. This is the Arctic at its best – the coming of spring on the east coast of Greenland.

'The timing of our arrival is perfect, for the thaw started just a few days ago and the first migrants have already arrived. Sanderling and snow bunting search for seeds on the snow, long-tailed duck dive through a narrow lead in the sea ice, long-tailed skuas stand expectant on prominent rocks. Barnacle geese have been here several days, the females already incubating their precious clutches on a nearby cliff. Surrounded as they are by a completely Arctic whiteness, their nesting strikes me as an optimistic gesture, an act of faith that the snow will eventually melt and the land provide.

'But the thaw itself is remarkable, the arrival of summer in the Arctic striking me as nothing far short of miraculous. From under the snow the frozen world comes to life. From apparently dead stems come leaves and flowers, insects buzz into action, rivers and lakes reform and the air is filled with song.'

So reads my diary for 6 June 1984, but the diary for 1974 says much the same. Almost ten years ago to the day, I had visited the place for the first time. The impression then, as now, was inspiring, and it became my ambition to return one day and make a complete film about the place. From this concept grew the trilogy of films on Arctic wildlife, and to remain true to my ambition, we had always had this location in mind for the land film. Although it was a gamble, I hoped this would be the ideal place to show what happens to wildlife during the seven weeks of high summer and twenty-four hours of daylight.

Mesters Vig lies some 200 kilometres north of Scoresby Sund on Greenland's east coast, but being in the High Arctic, the extreme climate makes wildlife susceptible to periodic 'crashes' in population, sometimes due to

93

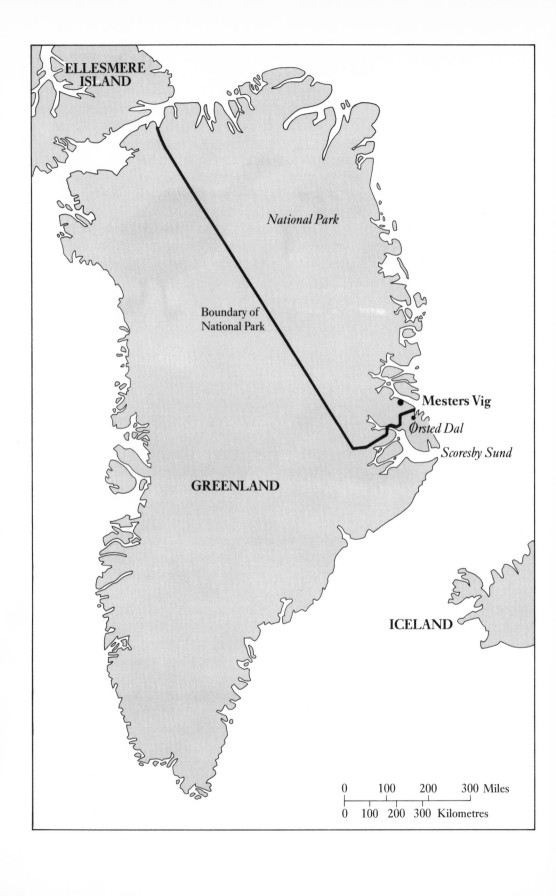

ELLESMERE
ISLAND

National Park

Boundary of
National Park

Mesters Vig

Ørsted Dal

Scoresby Sund

GREENLAND

ICELAND

| 0 | 100 | 200 | 300 Miles |
| 0 | 100 | 200 | 300 Kilometres |

severe weather conditions, at others due to natural cycles of productivity and decline. 1974 was one of the better years in the last few decades, but 1983 was really barren. However, there had been a few signs of improvement, and 1984 was tipped as a 'lemming year', something that only occurs once in every four years or so. Lemmings were vital to our film, for very few predators would breed without their bountiful presence.

So we had travelled more in faith than hope, for no one could know if it was to be a good year until the snow melted – if it melted! Sometimes it fails to do so until it is too late for virtually all the wildlife to breed. So for migrant wildlife, and for us, the journey north was indeed a gamble. It was also important to us that the place was still beautiful, for ten years is a long time.

Miraculously, at first glance there seemed little that was damaged or destroyed and there are few places on our beleaguered planet of which that can be said. Perhaps it has survived because man has yet to find something there that he wants? It is simply wonderful to find the same willow tree I filmed ten years ago; gnarled and twisted, but alive. The arctic hare still feeds where it did before, the barnacle goose stands sentinel on the same rock ledge, and the crevice where the snow bunting nested is still occupied. It is good to know that there are still places in the world where nothing changes.

Earlier that day we had flown north-west from Reykjavik, the capital of Iceland, and after two hours saw the pack ice drifting down the mountainous east coast of Greenland. My travelling companion was Mike Read, an experienced naturalist and photographer, whose skills would assist me with the task of trying to illustrate a typical High Arctic summer in just seven weeks. It was his first trip abroad and he was most impressed by the spectacular scenery, marvelling at the snow-capped mountains that disappeared into the clouds, and the glaciers that slither between them to the sea.

Greenland is a place of superlatives. It is the largest island in the world, has the largest and deepest glacier, and the national park in which Mesters Vig lies is also the largest in the world – over a million square kilometres. The Danes, who still retain sovereignty, run the weather station and airstrip at Mesters Vig: there is little else. They have to put up with several months of darkness and the lowest temperature recorded in 1983–4 was −48°C. Winter holds a firm grip until June, for even as we landed the ground was almost completely covered in deep snow. Most of it normally melts by mid-July, but the first snowfalls usually occur again as early as late September.

It is a short but glorious summer, a land where months of constant darkness give way to months of dazzling light. A land at one moment lifeless, at another teeming with migrants and a host of animals. Once the snow melts there is lots of food, and twenty-four hours of daylight in which to enjoy it. The sun often shines, and it can even be quite warm.

We hadn't come north purely for nostalgia but because East Greenland has a wide variety of wildlife, some of which would illustrate the strategies animals use for surviving the cold, and others the use they make of the Arctic summer. But if we were lucky we might also be able to illustrate the importance of lemmings to Arctic ecology, and on 7 June we saw the first of them,

Arriving over Greenland

Below: the Greenland ice-cap

Above: the camp near Mesters Vig and the view from it

Left: the start of the thaw

Below: filming a reluctant star — the lemming

popping their heads out of holes in the snow, and peering out of crevices in the rocks. The lemming hunters were there too, yelping display calls emanating from the hooked beaks of numerous deadly but delightful long-tailed skuas. Each bare patch of ground was defended by a pair, and their display is one of the most beautiful curving ballets to grace the skies. If there were enough lemmings the skuas would breed, and next day we saw two pairs mating.

As the thaw progressed it became clear that this was indeed a lemming year. Their heads popped up everywhere, and the snow was absolutely honeycombed with their tunnels. They had already chomped through sufficient vegetation to leave whole areas largely denuded. No wonder the Arctic is only able to support their delightful but numerous presence every four years or so. They seemed particularly fond of areas of *Dryas octopetala*, the pretty white and yellow mountain avens, for these occurred on gently sloping, well-drained ground.

Lemmings don't seem to like getting wet, and what moisture there is, in what is actually a cold desert, lies on the surface: the icy permafrost is just five centimetres down. The advantages of a well-drained site are then obvious, and not lost on the skuas. When enough bare ground is exposed by the melting snow, they lay their two eggs in a shallow scrape.

As soon as any lemming dared to leave its snow shelter and run off, the skuas were after it. There was usually no contest, the hapless rodent becoming a gift in a courtship display. However, one enterprising individual, when attacked by a skua, stood on its hind legs and displayed its impressive array of 'dentures', whereupon the skua flew off empty-handed. I gave a little cheer.

One useful behaviour trait the skuas did have was to attack any other predator in their territory; useful because we were alerted the moment we heard their alarm calls. With the lemmings numerous we were hoping that snowy owls would breed in East Greenland, but neither the skuas nor we saw one at Mesters Vig. We did see at least two arctic foxes virtually every night, and we would often be woken by the alarm calls of skuas as the foxes passed close to our tents.

The arctic foxes, just beginning to moult from their white winter pelage, added life to the landscape every time they appeared, for they are active opportunists that live life at a run. They are a contrast to every other mammal in the Arctic, which move slowly in winter to conserve energy, and to avoid overheating in the summer. All except the lemming, of course, which must run away from every predator in the Arctic, including the fox. The arctic fox has the finest insulating coat of all, but perhaps it has to hurry in order to investigate every potential source of food, otherwise it might starve. As you would expect, winter is the time of hardship, summer the time of plenty. The barnacle goose, nesting on inaccessible ledges on the cliffs, is well aware that it would become part of the 'plenty' if the fox had its way.

Barnacle geese, as with all arctic geese, are very pressed to complete their breeding cycle before winter returns, so they pair up in their winter quarters and arrive in East Greenland during May. As soon as the cliff ledges are clear of snow they lay their eggs. Nest preparation is minimal, largely the insulating down from the breast. The cliffs have two advantages: they provide protection from the foxes, and also tend to be the first places clear of snow.

The speed at which the snow melts is vital to all wildlife, but never more so than for the migrants who, having used up most of their energy reserves on the long journey north, need food fairly soon to survive. As they arrive, snow buntings, Lapland buntings, sanderling, turnstone and horned larks feed at the receding snow edge with a keenness which seems to border on desperation; a frenetic rushing hither and thither as the sun does its work. In reality they are trying to regain their condition as fast as possible so breeding can commence, and the snow edge is the best place to achieve this, revealing new food daily. Insects spend the winter in the drier vegetation on hilltops, and these wind-swept spots are the first to be exposed by the sun. So birds hunt for insects at the snow edge, and as the vegetation is exposed are joined by a wide variety of geese.

Paradoxically, *cold* is not the most important factor in the Arctic, for wildlife has adapted to it, but if *food* is not accessible, then birds and animals die. The Arctic thrives on stable conditions and migrants arrive on the same dates each year; problems arise only if there is a week or more of extra cold and the snow fails to melt.

Though finding food is the most important criterion for surviving in the Arctic, it does not mean that the cold is not a problem. Indeed, the far north is so challenging a place to live that most species of birds simply leave when the frosts return. Those that stay, or that drift south a little to avoid the worst of the winter darkness, have developed several adaptations to the cold. These species include the snowy owl, snow bunting, raven, black guillemot and ptarmigan.

Adaptations include changes in body size in the relative proportions of parts of the body, and in the use of insulation. As a general rule, birds breeding in the north tend to be larger than their counterparts in the south, one such species being the common wheatear, and this works because the larger the bird the smaller, relatively, is the surface available for heat loss. Another common method is to reduce the size of bodily extremities, especially bills in the case of birds, and ears, nose and tails in mammals.

Insulation has been improved in several ways. The feathers of Arctic birds are thicker and more numerous, and the downy bases of the body feathers are denser and therefore warmer. Snowy owls and ptarmigan have feathered legs and feet, while ravens and snow buntings, which do not, tend to crouch when feeding in order to improve insulation. Standing on one leg is also practised and ravens and snowy owls have developed thick pads on the undersides of their feet.

Several species of Arctic birds and mammals are white or pale coloured for at least some of the year, and this not only provides excellent camouflage but warmth, for white feathers are better insulators than coloured ones. This is because the colour pigment in a feather lies within its structure, so a white one remains hollow and air, of course, is a good insulator. Furthermore, a white object radiates less heat than a coloured one.

Male ptarmigan proclaims its territory

Far right: the female is well camouflaged

Male barnacle goose

Long-tailed skua

100

The moult of the ptarmigan is interesting. As the snow melts the female needs to be camouflaged to survive on her nest, so she changes to a brown summer plumage well before the male who, it is said, remains a conspicuous white in order to decoy any predator. Our diary of events highlighted some of the advantages and disadvantages of Arctic adaptations.

'17 June started as an ordinary day by East Greenland standards. Overnight, the snow buntings had laid their first egg. Down in the valley the long-tailed skuas were incubating; likewise the barnacle geese on a nearby crag. In the hills behind camp, a ptarmigan was also incubating. I climbed to a high meadow, hoping the geese would choose to feed there, for the backdrop was spectacular mountain scenery. After six hours, two eventually flew in, but by then the light was from the wrong angle and the heat haze viscous.

'I moved to the ptarmigan hide, hoping she would leave the nest for a feed, for previously I had watched her cover the eggs with infinite care as she edged backwards off the nest – a neat example of an anti-predator strategy. Unfortunately, all she did was pant in the heat, and sleep. Having moulted into her dark summer plumage, she was now absorbing so much heat that she appeared to be really suffering. Standing on guard nearby, the white male looked cool in his reflecting white. I left the hide at 10 p.m. and within half an hour it was snowing. Nothing serious we thought, it had happened before – just a gesture to remind us we really were in the High Arctic – so we turned in.

'Woken at 6 a.m. by the violent flapping of the tent, I looked outside and was greeted by horizontal snow and a complete white-out. The whole valley was transformed from midsummer to midwinter, the only visible land being the black crag on which the barnacle goose might still be incubating – but in this blizzard? Donning snow shoes and parka against the storm, I went out to investigate and, struggling to the ptarmigan, found the ledge on which she was nesting buried under two feet of snow. Whether she was still there I did not know, but I filmed the scene to contrast with yesterday's heat. On leaving the hide, my snow shoes had disappeared in a drift, so I floundered back to camp to await an improvement.

'Next day dawned bright and sunny, the weather seemingly ignoring the misdemeanours of the previous thirty hours. But the scene was spectacular – meadow, moor and mountain completely blanketed in crystalline white, all land forms blotted out. The pair of long-tailed skuas stood disconsolate on the spot where their eggs lay buried, then, as if to prove they are quite capable of withstanding the rigours of the Arctic, caught a lemming and restarted the courtship ritual all over again. Finding the snow shoes, I checked the barnacles' nest and the female sat unconcerned on her eggs with snow banked up to her down-lined nest. And the ptarmigan? Well, as the sun did its work first her head, then her back, miraculously appeared. She had sat there under the snow for forty hours, stoically ignoring the snowstorm – tough bird the ptarmigan.'

In the heat of the summer sun, the new snow melted and the setback to wildlife was short-lived. The winter snows continued to thaw and drips soon became trickles, gullies became streams, and as ice became water the scenery shimmered with a thousand starlight reflections.

As the snow slowly disappeared we regretted its loss, for the scenery was stunningly beautiful and we did not want it to change. It seemed perfect as it was, and we never tired of the view. Even when we finished work after midnight, we would still sit in the tent door for an hour or two, watching the layers of cloud and mist drift through the mountains. The sun never set, but merely circled us above the northern horizon.

We were sad to leave, but our plan had always been to head 65 kilometres south to a valley in Jameson Land called Ørsted Dal. The location would hopefully provide several sequences for our film, being well known for its variety of breeding mammals. There is also a good gyrfalcon site on the cliffs, and we hoped snowy owls would be breeding, but above all there are large barnacle goose colonies, and we hoped to film the fledging of their young.

We were not alone in our interest in the geese and in order to promote efficiency and save money, had arranged to join a scientific expedition from Ireland, led by David Cabot. David works on environmental matters for the Irish Government in Dublin but for years, as a hobby, has studied barnacle geese on their wintering grounds in Western Ireland and Scotland. The other members of David's team were Steve Newton, who carried out research for the Nature Conservancy Council on barnacle geese in Scotland, Richard Nairn, the director of the Irish Wildbird Conservancy, and Michael Viney, writer and artist, television producer, self-sufficiency expert and goose enthusiast.

Their principal objective was to investigate the breeding biology of the barnacle goose with a view to determining the factors which influence their productivity. The information gained would provide a better understanding of their population dynamics and assist in their conservation. The total population of barnacle geese in Greenland is small and vulnerable, for it has dropped by a quarter in five years and now numbers about 25,000. Some 200 pairs nest in Ørsted Dal, so on 20 June the six of us flew south in a large helicopter, weaving between dramatic snow-covered peaks whose glaciers and crevasses glinted in the afternoon sun.

David's expedition split into two teams of two, with Steve and Richard dropped by the helicopter on one side of the valley, and David and Michael Viney on the other. Their first task was to count the nesting colonies in the eastern part of the valley, then walk west on either side of the river which separated them, counting the geese on the way. As the valley is some 40 kilometres long and anything from four to eight kilometres wide, it struck me as a tough task. We bade them good luck, then flew up the valley to the largest goose colony of all and made a quick decision on where to camp; at £20 a minute flying time we could afford little hesitation. Cameras and camping gear were hurriedly unloaded, the relentless beating of the blades retreated over the mountain and the remote valley became silent once again.

Our first impressions were not encouraging, for we had landed in a swamp, the snow had all but melted, the scenery was comparatively dull, and there appeared to be no wildlife whatsoever. Once we had moved out of the marsh, set our tents, established radio contact with Mesters Vig and sat supping a mug of tea, our attitude improved.

103

The valley of Ørsted Dal and campsite above barnacle goose nesting cliffs

104

Campsite in the valley

By mid-July the valley was green

105

The valley was, on reflection, quite attractive, even impressive. Below us the gently undulating meadows dropped away to the river, which at that point was slow moving, wide and deep, and meandered through a sandy flood-plain with well-vegetated sand-dunes. I noted that it looked impossible to cross on foot. The river curved away to the east, and to the west the numerous braided channels of the river shimmered in the evening sun. Above them, the valley sides rose up to become dramatic peaks, and far beyond, the white light blazed off the ice-cap that crowns most of Greenland.

Two weeks before we had flown over those peaks and that vast land of ice beyond; the scenery was spectacular. Numerous blue and white glaciers had carved their way through the black mountains to the ocean, a process which provides the sea with its icebergs, and which, during the previous ice age, had shaped the valley in which we now camped. Beyond, the land comprised a vast dome of ice, 10 kilometres thick, stretching all the way to the Americas.

There was little sign of the ice age by the tents, for just two per cent of the valley floor was still snow-covered. Two large snow banks lay on either side and one trickled as it slowly melted – our water supply. Mountains on either side of the valley were still largely snow-covered, the ground between them coloured shades of rust-red, ochre and russet. Of the lush vegetation that would soon cover the valley floor there was still no sign; the ground was brown and bare.

Above us was the most impressive feature of all, the towering basalt cliffs upon which the barnacle geese nest. The sheer rock faces had been shattered by centuries of frost, and eroded into a series of narrow pinnacles many metres high; they stood cathedral-like against the sky. Each substantial ledge was covered with bright orange lichens, nourished by goose dropping nutrients. The geese have nested here for centuries and their cackling calls echoed down to us, joining the twittering of snow buntings and the trilling of dunlin.

In a small cave on the cliff above our tents, we could see the pair of gyrfalcons, the female at the nest, the male perched ice-white on a lofty spire. They had moved their site from the previous year's perfect filming spot, and when we tried to climb down to the new one we found it was quite impossible to reach. The friable cliffs fell away in great chunks as we tried to secure footholds in the frost-shattered debris and, in danger of our lives, we accepted defeat. It was a bitter disappointment.

However, in the valley below the apparently empty landscape began to come to life as our eyes became tuned to the scale. The marshes and tundra sprouted turnstone and sanderling, the rocks began to move and became musk oxen, long-tailed skuas bombed arctic foxes, lemmings peered out of their holes and, like apparitions, arctic hares hopped out of the snow. Seven appeared from one moraine, but on Ellesmere Island in Northern Canada herds of thirty or forty graze the tundra. We had considered visiting the island to film this spectacle, but with little else to attract us the rewards would not warrant the time or expense. Launching out on expeditions to remote locations is a costly business, especially in the Arctic.

Despite the continuous daylight, hares seemed to prefer to feed in the slightly more subdued light of the summer night, and that first evening one chose to graze in the marsh towards the river. I stalked it, and filmed its shuffling progress as it fed on the emerging shoots. It rested for a while, protected from the chill wind by its dense white fur. It is such effective insulation that in the heat of summer the hares move ever higher into the mountains, sitting on permanent snow banks for camouflage, and to cool off.

My subject woke eventually, stretched front and back legs in turn, and then suddenly, as if aware of my presence for the first time, ran off alarmed. This produced some lovely film, for in order to increase their height to spot predators, arctic hares run on their back legs, with body raised vertical. My 'star' did so for some 30 metres, splashing through the marsh with the snow-capped mountains behind, the spray sparkling gold in the midnight sun – a rewarding end to the day.

Ørsted Dal did have one curse, which also became a blessing – the wind. With the ice-covered sea one end and the ice-cap the other, the valley was a wind tunnel and, whether from east or west, the wind blew strongly and constantly. It tore at one's clothes, at the tents, shook the camera, blew the hides, even fractured the mind. There was no shelter from its unrelenting blast.

However, as the weather warmed up, the first mosquitoes appeared. I suggested to Mike in mock desperation that he must kill the first two before they bred, but of course we were well aware that millions of their colleagues had spent the winter as larvae in the silt at the bottom of ice-covered ponds, and now summer had arrived the war had started. One disgruntled northerner described the Arctic as 'nine months of winter and three months of bugs', and the biting black hordes are certainly irritating. We found it impossible to cook or eat without them flying into the food but gave up trying to remove them. I argued that if they tried to eat us, why shouldn't we eat them. Extra protein, I said, and with our supplies consisting of soya and monosodium glutamate they were almost welcome. Six mosquitoes to a slice of Ryvita was the ration, but if you were slow buttering it, you got a dozen. And the wind? That was a blessing because it blew the little bug - - - s away!

One fine afternoon our camp was approached by a herd of musk oxen, and frightening though they look with their box-like frames, shaggy black coats and large, curved horns, they are gentle, timid creatures and will tend to run away when approached. The wind was particularly strong so we used the tents both to shelter and to hide behind and filmed them feeding on the tundra plants. They were moulting their winter coats, and so strong was the wind that their dense fur and guard hairs were being blown off their backs like spindrift – they made a magnificent spectacle.

The herd had a young calf with them, born a month or two previously, and we were sad to see another drowned in the river a few days later. It was washed downstream to a sand-bank opposite the tents, and became the centre of attention for the district's ravens. However, the Ørsted Dal musk ox population could no doubt sustain such losses, for we counted more than 100 from the tent door one morning and the expedition census suggested the number in the whole valley was 181, split up into 38 herds.

*Above: musk oxen
were numerous in
Ørsted Dal*

Right: turnstone

108

Arctic hare

Below: arctic fox calls to its mate and a cub emerges from its earth

David Cabot and Michael Viney had now joined us and on 27 June the four of us carried out the long portage to the top of the cliffs in order to film the barnacle geese. We set up a 'satellite' camp above their nests and this involved three journeys back and forth up the 300-metre scree, a sweaty and at times hazardous struggle amongst the almost vertical loose boulders. At the top the view was stupendous. I felt as if we were on the roof of the world, with snowy mountains on every horizon, the vast ice-cap glistening to the west and our valley far below. Mike could be seen returning to base camp and looked diminutive. It brought home to me how insignificant we were in that vast terrain and how large an area we had to cover in order to find wildlife in the sparsely populated Arctic. He was to search for turnstone and sanderling nests in the valley whilst I tackled the barnacle geese on the cliffs.

Two days previously we had set a hide on a narrow ledge close to the only really suitable nest for filming. Both nest and hide were precariously perched on the edge of a 150-metre sheer drop, and below that there were 300 metres of steep broken boulder scree before the valley levelled off and sloped gently to the river about a kilometre away. This was the refuge to which the adult geese would have to lead their chicks, but first they had to hatch, and at 10.30 on the evening of 27 June the first egg was chipping.

The only previous observations of barnacle geese fledging suggested that they would leave the ledge within four hours of hatching, so I was on tenterhooks that evening. No one had ever witnessed the event close to, and for years it was believed that the parents carried the goslings down on their backs, or in their bills. It is now known that they jump, and such an event had never before been filmed. I did not want to miss it! I sat by the nest until two in the morning, but the hatch had still not taken place, so I risked a few hours' sleep in the tent on the clifftop, and returned to the hide at 6 a.m.

All was quiet for a while, but at 7.30 a.m. the female fidgeted about and revealed four fluffy and delightful goslings. The male was attentive and stood on guard, watching the chicks with interest. I was pleased, for within four hours I assumed I would have a unique sequence in the can. How wrong I was. Four hours passed with hardly a fidget from the adults and I had to sit motionless, keen to avoid alarming them. The deep silence of the Arctic was a problem, for it proved difficult to sit in a hide for hours without making the slightest sound. Have you any idea how noisy opening a Mars Bar is when you have barnacle geese asleep just six metres away?

I slipped out of the hide in mid-afternoon, and though it was only +3°C in the shade, there was real shirt-sleeve sunshine. On the clifftop it was +23°C – summer had arrived. I grabbed a quick tin of sardines and a mug of tea, admired the valley below, which appeared to be turning green as I watched, then dived back into the hide to continue the watch.

In the evening the chicks took their first walk, staggering around the rock ledge as the adults kept an eye on the predatory glaucous gulls and ravens that circled the cliffs. The chicks appeared to have progressed a little, but the adults cannot wait several weeks for their wings to grow. They are hungry, keen to reach the marshes below, for there is no food around the nest. The chicks peered over the cliff edge for the first time, calling with alarm, and I grew nervous too, sharing the anxiety the parents so obviously showed for the perils ahead, not just the chicks' momentous 'free fall' down the cliff, but the climb through the scree, the threat of foxes, the weeks of growth to the flying stage, then, if they survive all that, the 3000-kilometre migration to Scotland. It seems sad that a gun may be waiting for them on Islay, just because they like to eat grass. You would think man would be generous enough to spare a few acres of grass for these Arctic travellers and extend a hand of welcome, but the profit motive reigns supreme.

The family of geese seemed to view the prospect from the ledge with considerable fear and apprehension, as well they might. Even an experienced rock climber might view the sheer drop with some trepidation, let alone a day-old, 10-centimetre-high gosling. The female became quite neurotic, strutting around with neck stretched taut, craning this way and that, like a demented ostrich. The decision not to jump was received with such delight that they all rushed back to the nest and sank down with a visible sigh of relief.

So the day passed, minutes of hesitation interspersed with hours of slumber, and by midnight, unable to sustain concentration any longer, I radioed Mike down in the valley to come and relieve me from the vigil.

29 June was again fine, and on entering the hide after breakfast I noticed that a pair of geese on a ledge across the gully had a chick that looked like jumping. The drop was several hundred feet, the shot would be terrific, but when the gosling did finally leap out into space a few hours later, it immediately fell into a crevice and was killed.

However, the excited calls of the adults infected our own pair, and their visits to the edge became more frequent. Finally, at 9.30 p.m., the adults led the chicks to the very edge and the female, after much heart-rending indecision and anxious calling, slid off the ledge, followed hesitantly by the male. The chicks milled around, calling pathetically, peered over the edge, huddled together again, then, as if encouraged by this fraternal behaviour, jumped one after another. However, the smallest chick was left behind and it wandered back and forth, torn between the fear of the fall and the circling glaucous gulls that threatened to snap it up. After a couple of minutes it went to the edge and, screwing up its courage, leapt out into the abyss.

I climbed out of the hide after our own forty-eight-hour ordeal and walked stiffly up to the tent to watch for the family in the valley below. What a joy it was to stand out in the open with the sun on my back, looking down on the marshes, the ribbons of green spreading out, nourished by the water from the hills. At midnight they glistened in the sunshine, a fairy-tale land of snowy mountains and silver streams.

I eventually spotted our family just below the scree. All four chicks had made it – I smiled with pleasure. They headed for the river, where a herd of musk oxen were being taunted by an arctic fox. The fox was having fun, for like a playful puppy it would gambol in front of its chosen victim until the musk ox was goaded into chasing it, then run just ahead until the musk ox tired and stopped. The fox then selected a new 'playmate', and the game

Mountain avens

Top: arctic poppy
Above: saxifrage
(left) and arctic
campion

Left: Lapland
rhododendron

113

continued for several minutes until eventually a truce was called and the fox wandered off. It was an amusing end to a memorable day.

On returning to the valley next morning, we discovered the whole area had become covered with flowers, transformed during our absence into a magic garden. There were carpets of white mountain avens, yellow poppies, white heather, crimson, yellow, red, white and purple saxifrage, lousewort, pink primulas, orange marigolds, moss campion.

All these flowers had started their cycle of growth as the snow melted, responding to the sunshine and available moisture, a commodity that is normally so scarce in this cold desert. Less than a metre below the surface, the land remains frozen throughout the year, but this layer of permafrost ensures the moisture remains on the surface, and available to the plants.

With the flowers came the insects, and by early July the valley fairly hummed with them, not just flies but bumblebees and butterflies, the northern clouded yellow and polar fritillary being particularly attractive. Both species have hairy abdomens, not to keep warm but to ensure they stay dry, particularly in the winter when they literally freeze under the snow. So long as they are dry they will survive, and July is the season of awakening.

Each morning we rose to the sound of rain, but the pattering on the tent was in fact mosquitoes – millions of them. The air seemed to comprise 50% oxygen and 50% mossies and they formed the only clouds in the lovely summer weather. Temperatures rose to +28°C, the equivalent of 82°F, warm by any standards, but sunbathing was out, the blood-suckers saw to that.

The days slipped by as we completed various film sequences, most of which related to the flush of insects. Snow buntings fed their young on the numerous crane-flies, turnstone and sanderling chicks hatched, long-tailed skuas hunted the fledglings, and barnacle goose families made their way upriver to Primula Pond to moult. It was a case of collecting the last few remaining pieces of the jigsaw, and our frenetic activity was similar to that of the arctic foxes. They rushed hither and thither collecting and caching food, for it is not the summer feast that determines their survival but the ice-bound winter. 'Be prepared' is also their motto. We put food out for the foxes in order to try to tame them a little, but this was eaten by the lemmings. Justice was done we thought. Then the foxes ate the porridge oats put out for the lemmings – not so fair!

We climbed up the scree each day, pursuing the foxes that had by now come to recognise the excited calls of the barnacle geese to mean that a meal was on its way down. The geese synchronise their hatch and fledging in order to avoid such predatory search patterns developing, for by 'saturating the market' they prevent the fox from killing them all. But the late jumpers suffered heavy losses. We filmed the chicks' 'free-falls' from below, saw them survive the drop, then watched helplessly as the foxes moved in and grabbed them. The little barnacle goose adults are no match for the arctic fox, and fled when approached. Those goslings that survived the fox were then stranded in the scree, and also succumbed. The whole process was exasperating to watch – it all seemed so futile. Gosling mortality in our colony was 60–70%, but

114

David's research indicated a slightly better rate for the total of 188 pairs that nested in the valley. Of the eighty-one chicks that were observed jumping, thirty-nine made it to the river.

The arctic foxes certainly did well in that year of plenty, and while we were filming at one of their earths we saw both lemmings and goslings brought to their young. On the arrival of the female with food, the ground would explode with competitive cubs, and when they were not scrabbling for a share of the food, they spent hours rough-and-tumbling with apparent delight. There were eight in all, ample evidence that it was a lemming year.

With the pace of life so rapid in July, we had found it difficult to keep ahead and film each event. The task was hard on the muscles, and even harder on the footwear. My climbing boots had become frayed and split and leaked water like colanders. The valley floor had become one large morass, so our work revolved around three pairs of socks – one on, wet – the second pair washed and wet – the third pair drying. We should have developed webbed feet!

On 17 July the weather finally broke and rain beat down relentlessly for almost three days. Grey mist hung low over green meadows, the layers of moisture lending an air of mystery and sadness to the valley. It was very beautiful, but the rain signalled the end of the brief Arctic summer. Autumn had arrived and winter seemed to be waiting in the hills. We were pleased to have finished most of our filming, though in such a rich place we could never really finish. We had done our best in the time available, we had even had some success, but at the end of seven weeks one major disappointment remained – we had not filmed snowy owls.

*Female snowy owl
landing near nest*

THE OWL AND THE LEMMING

The small island of Igloolik lies almost 70° North at the top end of Foxe Basin and just eight kilometres from Melville Peninsula on the Canadian mainland to the east. On a clear day, the mountains of Baffin Island can be seen to the north and west. The first impressions on landing are not very encouraging – it appears to be little more than a featureless, low-lying gravel heap. But like many desert locations – and the High Arctic is as much a desert as the Sahara when judged by annual precipitation – the attractions are more subtle and mature gently with knowledge. But it was not the scenery that had brought Hugh and myself to Igloolik in the first place, it was the recent report that snowy owls were nesting there in good numbers, unlike at most of the more regular locations throughout the Canadian Arctic.

Snowy owls are not particularly rare in the Arctic. They are in fact familiar birds in many locations and, with their large size and dazzling white plumage, are easy to spot even from a long distance. They use traditional nesting sites on the ground, which are fairly simple to find as decades of use build up a prominent, well-fertilised mound, marked by luxuriant vegetation and old feathers.

On the face of it then, our decision to include the complete breeding cycle of this magnificent bird of prey in our film series should not have presented any great difficulty, at least as far as choosing a suitable location was concerned. But the fact is that snowy owls belong to a highly mobile population and can travel great distances before deciding where to nest. Their final choice seems to depend, quite understandably, upon one vital factor, a plentiful supply of their staple diet – lemmings.

So, by finding out which traditional owl area is experiencing one of the four-yearly (or so) population explosions of these little rodents, it should be possible to say for certain that the owls will be nesting there. But it's never that easy, for lemmings begin their breeding cycle under the snow cover, and it's not until early June, when the melt begins, that one can get even a vague indication of likely numbers. The whole situation was beautifully summed up by an experienced Arctic biologist, Dr Stephen Maclean, when we rang him at the Institute of Arctic Biology in Fairbanks, Alaska. His first comment was, 'I've got it wrong so many times in the past that I've lost all credibility, even with myself!'

Of course, Dr Maclean went on to give us some very useful information, as did all the other biologists and local wildlife officers that I spoke to in far-flung locations throughout the Arctic, during a desperate last-minute ring-round while Hugh was on his own filming caribou calving in the Canadian Barren Lands. The resultant telex sent to Hugh in Yellowknife on 13 June paints the picture nicely:

> FROM: MIKE SALISBURY, NHU BBC BRISTOL
>
> TO: HUGH MILES, C/O YELLOWKNIFE INN, YELLOWKNIFE NWT CANADA
>
> NEXT TRIP A PROBLEM AS LEMMING AND SNOWY OWL NUMBERS ERRATIC AND VERY LOW AT ALL OUR PLANNED LOCATIONS: CAMBRIDGE BAY, COPPERMINE, CORAL HARBOUR, SOUTHAMPTON ISLAND AND BARROW. BEST BET IS WITH DR NORMAN NEGUS ON IGLOOLIK ISLAND. HE REPORTS LEMMINGS VERY PLENTIFUL AND SNOWY OWLS AND JAEGERS ACTIVE AND COMMON. SOME NESTS REPORTED BY INUIT HUNTERS AT NEARBY MOGG BAY, PLUS DUCKS, SNOW GEESE, MANY WADERS AND DIVERS. SCENICS MORE FLAT AND ORDINARY THAN DESIRED, BUT LEMMINGS MAY FORCE ISSUE.
>
> WILL RING, CHEERS, MIKE SALISBURY

So it was that on the evening of 29 June, Hugh and I sat in Dr Andy Rode's house in the small Inuit settlement of Igloolik and discussed the practicalities of filming snowy owls. Andy is the director of the Eastern Arctic Research Centre, a facility of remarkably modern laboratories housed in a tall, mushroom-shaped building which dominates the otherwise low-lying huddle of wooden houses. Also with us were Norman Negus and Pat Berger, biologists from the University of Utah in Salt Lake City, who were doing lemming research and using Andy's laboratory as a base.

The conversation confirmed that there were plenty of lemmings around of both common species: the collared lemming, which we could expect to find on the drier hillsides and raised beaches, and the brown lemming which lives on the wetter sedge meadows and seemed to be building up in great numbers for what they thought might be a 'peak' year. Snowy owls had been seen hunting over the island on several occasions but none had nested, so the advice was still to camp for a few days at Mogg Bay, about 15 kilometres over the ice. It was possible to get there by skidoo and sledge, but the ice would be very wet and bumpy for the camera equipment so we planned to fly over the next day. In the meantime, we collected together our food, camping gear, radio and inevitable gun, kindly loaned to us by Andy, and also arranged with Norman and Pat to film lemmings with them in detail on our return.

By 4 p.m. the next day, everything was ready for departure when a radio message came through from the pilot of the Twin Otter we had chartered to say that he had made several low passes over Mogg Bay, couldn't find anywhere safe to land and was sorry but must return to base. Disappointed by this news, we had resigned ourselves to an uncomfortable sledge journey when, as if on cue, a helicopter landed in the middle of the settlement. The government geologists on board were happy to have a short break from flying, so the pilot agreed to a brief charter with us. He judged, however, that to get both of us and our mountain of equipment over to Mogg Bay would require two trips. Hugh left on the first run with all the camera gear. He would have to make a snap decision as to where to position the camp as there was no spare time or fuel for a recce. Forty minutes later I climbed on board for the second run and as we landed could see Hugh standing on top of a ridge of bare shingle holding three fingers in the air and pointing animatedly in a southerly direction. I knew this signal meant three snowy owl nests and felt greatly relieved that the whole exercise began to look worth the high cost of getting there.

As the frenetic sound of the helicopter faded into the distance a symphony of bird song took over. Horned larks, phalaropes and plovers were prominent, backed by the eerie calls of red-throated loons, the chortle of long-tailed ducks, and the urgent, high-pitched distress cries of a pair of jaegers who seemed to find our arrival in their pristine wilderness a cause for concern. The vast lonely beauty of the place had a profound effect – overwhelming in a way, almost too perfect to be possible; a feeling that occurred time and time again in the Arctic and a mood which we both agreed must be conveyed in our films.

The nearest snowy owl nest was on top of our ridge, about two kilometres to the south, while another was a kilometre further on beyond a wet sedge meadow where several greater snow geese were also nesting. The female owls on their nests stood out clearly against the grey shale, and the brilliant white males could easily be spotted coursing the rough vegetation for lemmings. Hugh had chosen well and we decided to pitch camp right there. It was not sheltered, but did provide an excellent vantage point.

To the east, a series of raised beaches, many with small lakes in between, ran parallel with the coastal edge of the sea ice. To the north, the Lailor river surges to the sea, and to the west, beyond a stretch of continuous, lake-dappled sedge meadows, a range of low mountains, still largely snow-covered, glint like the skyline of a mysterious distant city. By 7.30 p.m. the tent and radio aerial were up and, despite a chill north wind, we got warm fetching large rocks for the mud flaps and guy ropes to stop the tent blowing away. Inside, Hugh's camera boxes made a good cooking table and there was ample room for two camp beds. The light was still good, so we gathered the two hides and set off for the owl nests.

The female on the nearest nest flew off when we were about a kilometre away and we quickened our pace so that the eggs would be without warmth for as short a time as possible. It turned out that there were only four eggs in the shallow nest. Perhaps it was a late season and she was still laying, for seven to nine is a more normal number.

Male snowy owl

Below: black-bellied plover (left) and collared lemming

Far right: male king eider

120

The choice of camera angle was slightly above and 20 metres to the north, so that the bird should fly towards the lens when returning to the nest. It didn't take long to erect the hide and to weigh down the canvas edges with rocks before backing off rapidly to give the female a chance to return as soon as possible. She had her piercing yellow eyes fixed on us the whole time from another ridge about 250 metres away, but now we were glad to see some short tentative flights back towards her nest. The pure white male watched us with equal interest from a nearby mound. They really are most stunning birds, particularly in that magnificent, wild setting.

As we made our way across the meadow towards the second nest, the first female eventually returned, although she was still very nervous. We stopped for a moment to inspect a small rock that was caked with droppings and surrounded by owl pellets full of lemming bones: obviously a favourite perch for many years. The position we chose for the other hide gave a view pointing up towards the owl nest, with a snow goose nest nearby. The female owl glowered at us from a surprisingly short distance and returned more quickly than the first one to her seven eggs. Possibly she was an older bird, and less anxious.

By the time we had had something to eat, the owls seemed to be acclimatising quite well, so we decided to move the first hide another six metres closer before going to bed and it was midnight as we walked back to our tent for the second time. The pale orange sun sat just above the horizon in a clear strip of sky, providing a dramatic light for the day's finale as a long-tailed jaeger hovered for a few seconds over a nearby lemming burrow. It swooped down for the kill and the hapless little rodent was caught and swallowed in one swift, conclusive scene.

The following morning, during a circular scan with binoculars from our campsite, we were able to count over twenty snowy owl nests. Admittedly they show up well at a distance, so our view covered a relatively wide area – perhaps 10 square kilometres or so; but nevertheless the fact that so many *were* nesting indicated that the lemming population was indeed as high as Norman and Pat had predicted.

Research has shown that the number of lemmings which first appear at snow melt back in early June determines whether snowy owls bother to breed at all. The male catches and brings lemmings to the female while she busies herself around the prospective nesting site. He gives them to her in much the same way as he will later on if she is brooding eggs, while she greets him with a strange grunting call and some energetic head bobbing. If lemmings are plentiful and the male can bring in a steady supply of food 'presents', the female will become receptive to mating and will then settle down to lay. Even then it seems that the number of eggs she will finally produce is linked to the number of lemmings the male can bring to the nest.

So there we were, thankful to be in a location chosen that year by so many snowy owls; our advice had certainly been good. We moved the hide even closer to the first nest after breakfast, but decided against filming until the

evening. For one thing it would give the owls more time to settle and for
another we had been told that both species of lemming tend to hide in their
burrows until late afternoon, when they come out in numbers for a night of
feeding. It also gave us an ideal chance to go for a long walk around the area to
pinpoint other subjects to film and to enjoy the beauty of the place.

The prominent features of this landscape, apart once more from the
impression of a vastness unspoilt by modern man's polluting influence, are the
dry stony ridges snaking along the contour lines to the wide arch of the
horizon. These 'raised' beaches, built up by the force of waves and ice, are an
indication of a retreating sea which, over thousands of years, has left on land a
series of former shorelines. Here at Mogg Bay, they stretch, bank after bank,
across 30 kilometres of fairly flat terrain towards the nearest mountains. Being
natural embankments, they are very well drained and bare of any vegetation
except in small pockets or folds where moisture and enough nutrients are
trapped for mosses, lichens and dwarf Arctic plants to grow. Here also were
the holes of the collared lemming.

Raised beaches make fine, dry walkways but, because they follow the
curve of an ancient shore, eventually lead you away from your destination. We
were trying to head for the mouth of the Lailor river, so now had to cut across
the sedge meadows which lie between each ridge. By contrast, the lush areas of
green were very wet underfoot, the water held there by the surrounding banks
and by the permafrost below. Shallow ponds and lakes of crystal-clear water
dappled the sedge land and here we began to see and hear some of the more
spectacular visiting birds.

We were struck by the brilliant colours of the breeding plumage of species
which in Britain we see only in their drab winter garb. Phalaropes for instance
– which we call 'grey', but in Canada are known as 'red' because of their vivid
colour. In several places these lovely birds were twirling around in the water,
stirring up larvae and other small creatures from the sediment. There were
many common turnstone, known here as 'ruddy' in description of the
vividly-patterned male's beautiful dark-red head and neck. A black-bellied
plover (our 'grey' plover) strutted off, calling in alarm as we walked past.
Red-throated loons were nesting by the lakes and feeding in the water, and
king eider ducks were also plentiful, the drakes performing their 'raised-neck'
ritual display and showing off their extravagant colours – the scarlet bill and
brilliant orange facial flash contrasting with a pastel-green and light grey head.
Numerous smaller birds became obvious in time – snow and Lapland buntings, horned larks and little groups of stints, and Baird's sandpipers with their
strange frog-like calls. Overhead, skeins of snow geese flew between their
feeding and nesting areas.

Some areas of the damp meadow were close-cropped as if a lawn mower
had been at work and, on looking more closely, we could see they were also
sprinkled with a carpet of tiny droppings. A network of runs and holes made it
obvious that enormous numbers of brown lemmings had been at work here –
feeding away under the snow cover until it had melted. At this moment they
seemed to be hiding in their burrows until the lower light of evening, although

*Overleaf: the
sea ice breaks up*

no less than three species of jaeger – arctic, pomarine, and the beautiful long-tailed variety – swooped around against the mackerel sky, in anticipation, we presumed, of a lemming supper.

When we reached the mouth of the river, surging dramatically with meltwater from the distant snow-covered hills, Hugh couldn't resist unfolding his rod and casting a brief spinner. At this time of year, arctic char make their way in great numbers from the freshwater inland lakes to the sea. We took a circular route back to our tent – empty-handed, I ought to mention – and passed on the way the remains of several groups of stone huts lying behind the top of an ancient raised beach. From what we had read, it seemed likely that these were built by Eskimos of the so-called Dorset culture, particularly strong in the Igloolik area between about 800 BC and AD 900.

The remains we looked at would have been the winter homes of these people, built half-submerged into the ground for extra protection and heated by a crescent-shaped, soapstone blubber-lamp. On such sites have been found the most delicately-carved ivory figures, depicting human activity and local wildlife, some less than two centimetres high and considered by many experts to be the most exquisite examples of Eskimo art ever produced; paradoxical for the people who in modern Inuit folklore live on as the Tunit. They were a race of mighty giants and prodigious hunters who could 'pull home across the ice a dead walrus as if it were the smallest seal', but who were quarrelsome, easily angered and prone to the vicious rivalry and fights with neighbouring groups which eventually caused their decline. By about AD 1000 they had been absorbed or destroyed by the smaller, more inventive Thule Eskimos, who swept across the area eastwards from Alaska with their dog teams and their kayaks.

Quite apart from any historical interest, the ancient site was fascinating to us as an illustration of the scarcity of plant nutrients in that polar desert. The village had probably not been used for a thousand years and yet, in great contrast to the otherwise totally bare grey pebbles, there was, in that immediate area, a dense carpet of mosses, lichens, arctic willow, saxifrage, mountain avens and other beautiful plants in great profusion – still fertilised, no doubt, by the ancient leftovers of a million meals.

It had been a rewarding tour; we had pinpointed the nests of various species and seen good locations – like our Dorset hut remains – where we could illustrate aspects of Arctic botany; but now, as the evening sun lowered in a perfect clear sky, it became the moment to try for our first snowy owl footage. As we walked along the ridge towards the nest, the female flew off to a nearby rock. In the shallow peat depression lined with soft white underfeathers and shreds of lichen there were now five large cream eggs. She watched us film her precious clutch and then move the camera into the canvas hide. Once Hugh was settled and hidden, for what we expected would be a five- or six-hour stay, I moved purposefully away from the hide and strolled in full view back to camp. We trusted that, like other birds, our snowy owl wasn't very good at counting and would presume all intrusion of her privacy to be over. Hugh describes what he saw from his close-up position:

'The moment Mike was sufficient distance away, the female took off and flew directly towards me. Her broad white wings beat slowly, but she moved through the air with speed and had to spread her wings and tail fully in order to brake when she reached the nest. This posture revealed a large pink "brood patch" between her feathered legs, the skin devoid of feathers in order to assist the transfer of heat to the eggs. As she landed close to the nest, she stared at the hide with her great sulphur-yellow eyes and didn't like what she saw.

'Though we had taken two days to place the hide in a series of moves, each one closer to the nest than the last, we had not risked putting in a dummy lens in the form of a bottle in case she took offence. If we kept her off her five white eggs for too long in the chill wind, their development might suffer. I was now anxious that she should sit on those eggs, but she stared into my lens with a fierceness which reached my own retina. I shrunk mentally, but dared not move a muscle and, once satisfied, she walked back to the nest in an ambling gait and settled to incubate in a series of shuffles and wriggles and a shake of the feathers. She had flecks of brown on her back and breast, and looked very matronly with her white plumage fluffed up for added insulation.

'She half-closed her eyes in the evening sun and, thinking she'd relaxed, I tried to move the lens slightly to adjust the shot. Five centimetres was too much. She gave me an eye-piercing stare, stood up unhurriedly and flapped noiselessly off to a knoll in the valley just below. She landed, watched by the male, who was perched on a nearby rock outcrop. Thinking her departure from the nest was an invitation to mate again, he flew over to the female, landed on her back and, with much flapping of wings, did so. As she was still laying, he had to ensure that each egg was fertilised so mated frequently. His pure white plumage stood out strikingly from her drabber hue, and, though he was markedly smaller than the female, he looked like a shining jewel amongst the dull browns of the marshy desert.

'The female returned to the nest hesitantly, flying several passes across the front of the hide before she would land. After five minutes of scrutiny she decided that I posed no threat and returned to the nest. I breathed a sigh of relief and she went to sleep. We had made an encouraging start.'

Over the next two days the weather was dry but with variable cloud, so between breakfast and suppertime we fell into a pattern of filming other nests and bird activity whenever the light was good enough, before leaving Hugh in the snowy owl hide for the whole evening until about midnight or beyond.

We particularly liked a horned lark's nest, which was hidden amongst a clump of lemon-yellow lichen and pale gold avens quite near to our tent. The tiny moss-lined cup contained seven morsels of animated fluff, with gaping orange mouths that would open in unison whenever one of the adults returned with a beakful of tasty caterpillars. The camouflage colours were so perfect that even when we knew we were staring straight at the correct spot it was possible to believe it had vanished. Many are the small-scale details like this which, when compared with the spectacular vastness of their setting, help to make the tundra such a memorable place.

To appreciate the subtle adaptations of Arctic plants to this unforgiving desert environment also requires a detailed, lying-down approach; for, as protection against the cold and the abrasive winds, everything hugs tightly to the ground. Various species of arctic willow, for instance, instead of growing upwards like a normal tree, spread their branches out along the ground. But the growth rate is so slow that a specimen covering an area only a metre across, and with branches merely the thickness of a man's finger, might be centuries old. Dwarf forms of heather, fireweed, lupin, bistort, buttercup and many other recognisable southerly species, together with compact cushions of saxifrage, dryas and moss campion, form low-lying carpets of unexpectedly brilliant colour. With a maximum height of only four to six centimetres in most places, these layers of vegetation provide a microclimate warmer than the surrounding air, sometimes by as much as 20°C, within which buds can form and insects flourish. Hairy leaves and stems also help to reduce desiccation and the cooling effect of the wind.

*Arctic willow –
the tallest tree
in the Arctic*

*Below and right:
Arctic blossoms
in the summer sun*

129

For ten months of the year growth is virtually at a standstill, leaving only two months – mid-June to mid-August – to run rapidly through the entire growth and reproduction cycles. Because the summer, in exceptional instances, can be even shorter than that, most of these perennial plants can extend their reproduction over several seasons if necessary. Arctic willows and saxifrage in any case form new buds in autumn which lie dormant under the winter snow cover, providing essential food for resident animals like ptarmigan and lemming.

We noticed how owl nesting sites, or even regularly used rock perches, encouraged an unusual flourish of plant growth in much the same way as the ancient garbage had around the Inuit ruins. Fertilised by centuries of droppings, a vivid orange lichen covered the rocks, while all the regular plants and some less common ones grew taller all around. The extra vegetation tended to attract more lemmings, which in turn produced more droppings, which encouraged jaegers and owls to hunt or nest, fertilising the area with yet more droppings, and so on and so on – a self-perpetuating mini-oasis.

On the evening of 3 July, after a brief game of cricket with snow shovel and tennis ball, Hugh went into the hide as usual, hoping desperately to capture on film the male owl passing a freshly-caught lemming to the brooding female – something which up to now the male had been too nervous to do. His best hunting period seemed to be the two hours before and after midnight, so Hugh might be in for a long wait.

Meanwhile, I washed the dishes by the tent entrance and revelled in the eerie calls of some red-throated loons on a nearby lake. I couldn't help thinking how lucky we were to experience a place like this, where no man-made cacophony interrupts the natural sounds. It turned out to be a thought worth savouring while the chance was there, for, like most delights, it was about to end. Hugh again takes up the story.

'I had been in the hide several hours with no action, when the familiar beat of a helicopter became ever more insistent and, looking out of the rear of the hide, I saw it land by our distant tents. What could this mean? I radioed Mike with the walkie-talkie and asked what was happening. His reply crackled back, "The ice is breaking up, Hugh. We'll need to be lifted out by chopper. Has the male performed? They want us to leave now. Over." I told him I hadn't finished the sequence yet. Mike replied, "Understand, but the chopper is leaving the area in the morning. They will return at 6 a.m. That's the best they can do – sorry. Over." The owls better hurry up; for we had only seven hours to finish filming and strike camp. There wouldn't be much sleep tonight!

'It was midnight when the male first visited the nest with a lemming, but the transfer to the female was untidy and I sat it out in the hope of another feed. One and a half hours later the male flew in again, carrying a lemming by the scruff of the neck. On his approach, the female lowered her head and made soft begging calls and, on landing, the male gently passed the lemming to her, gave me a moment's intense stare and then drifted off into the night. The female threw back her head, opened her capacious mouth and swallowed the lemming in one gulp, closing her eyes in apparent relish. We had finally filmed the main sequence we had come for. I called Mike up to help strike the two hides, which just left time to grab two hours of contented sleep before the helicopter shattered the peace yet again.'

After the pristine wilderness of Mogg Bay, the rubbish-strewn gravel surrounds of Igloolik village seemed sordid by comparison. We nevertheless enjoyed travelling out to other parts of the island over the next few days, joining Norman Negus and Pat Berger at some of their lemming study areas. Extensive 'lawns' of closely-cropped sedge, carpets of droppings, and numerous nest bundles showed all the signs of a massive population of brown lemmings, but one of the first things Norman and Pat did was to quash any thoughts of mass lemming suicide.

The popular belief that these little animals periodically gather in enormous numbers, throw themselves over cliff edges and swim off to their deaths is no more than a fairy story. Numbers do of course fluctuate, and these brown lemmings of the North American Arctic, and Norway lemmings in particular, build up phenomenal populations during peak years. When this happens, they can, and sometimes do, literally eat themselves out of house and home; nibbling the available vegetation to its very roots. Lack of food forces them to migrate to other areas to find more, but often neighbouring patches are already eaten bare and it's then that animals might die in their thousands through sheer starvation. If they happen to be near a lake or river, they do sometimes go into the water in an attempt to reach fresh pastures and, although like most rodents they are strong swimmers, in a weakened state they might also perish in great numbers. What they *never* do is to cast themselves over the edge of a high cliff in an act of heroic unselfishness – to save their species from extinction! It's an idea left only for films of fiction, not of fact.

What is far more interesting is the work being done by Norman and Pat on the ways in which the environment might trigger the breeding response in brown lemmings and cause these population 'highs'. It was always thought, for instance, that increases in daylight length and temperature were alone responsible for the start of breeding. But Norman and Pat have identified a chemical substance which is produced in the fresh shoots of grasses and sedges as they sprout under the snow and which, when eaten by male and female lemmings, seems to bring on sexual activity. The chemical 6-Methoxybenzoxazolinone (or 6-MBOA for short) also seems to affect the frequency of litters, and the number of young produced in each. So, at the beginning of the season, when the vegetation contains a lot of 6-MBOA, litters are large and frequent, and females become sexually mature in only three to four weeks, whereas later on in the season when new plant growth diminishes, the animals respond with a slowing down and eventually a complete halt to their reproduction. This is just another example of the neat way in which green plants hold the key to all life: in this case, not only the numbers of brown lemmings themselves but, because they rely on them for food, the breeding success of snowy owls, arctic foxes and the three species of jaeger.

Above: female
snowy owl

Right: female
with young

132

Female at its nest site

Martin with owl chick

133

Pat and Norman have found, however, that the collared lemming, living on the drier ridges and knolls, prefers a more varied diet, including arctic willows and evergreen shrubs like mountain avens which, bearing last year's leaves and buds, can be browsed upon before the new growth of the current season. The thought is that this habit makes collared lemmings less reliant on chemical plant cues to start breeding in spring: day length and temperature, in their case, being more important. It could also explain the relative stability of collared lemming numbers compared to the enormous population peaks and troughs of the brown variety.

In order to test these theories in the controlled conditions of the laboratory it was necessary to capture animals from the wild and start a number of breeding colonies. For us this was a great advantage, as we felt that the only way to film lemming breeding activity under the snow was in captivity. Consequently, before we left Igloolik, we arranged with Norman Negus for the shipment of two pairs of collared lemmings to Britain. They would have to remain in quarantine for six months at Ravensden Zoo, but thereafter we could film them at our leisure.

During our earliest discussions about the Arctic series, Hugh and I had decided to try very hard to film all the animals in the wild, rather than resorting to captive situations. We felt that even though close-ups of polar bears and white whales in aquarium tanks, or arctic wolves in a zoo enclosure, could well be more dramatic than anything we might achieve on location, we ought to compensate for this by trying to give our viewers an even stronger idea of the beauty, the vastness and the rigour of the Arctic environment, within which each animal has to survive. Large portraits and intimate behaviour, yes, but only when included in very wide-angle shots to set the scene properly.

Now, on delivering the lemmings to our colleague, wildlife cameraman Owen Newman, we were breaking our own rules for the first – and I'm glad to say the *only* – time in *Kingdom of the Ice Bear*. Our justification was the difficulty of showing how lemmings behave in their runs and nests under the snow. Perhaps in the future someone will prove that it *can* be done in the wild, and we shall be hoisted on our own petard; but in the meantime, Owen started to breed lemmings in earnest and to build numerous sets – both of real English snow and the false polystyrene variety – for them to live and be filmed in. Over a year, the colony built up to thirty or so individuals and he was able to shoot some most effective scenes, including mothers suckling their very young babies.

Being on the diet of so many Arctic predators perhaps resigns lemmings to a docile frame of mind. Certainly Owen found them to be most charming and good-natured animals, the only rodents he has so far encountered which don't immediately try to sink their sharp incisors as far into your finger as possible!

On 14 July 1984, myself, Martin Saunders and his assistant Jeremy Humphries returned to Igloolik in the hope of filming snowy owl chicks of various ages to complete the sequence started over a year ago. Andy Rode cheerfully supplied us with accommodation and transport again, and was soon showing us two nest sites right there on the island, which he hoped would save us the expensive journey to Mogg Bay.

Lemming numbers were even higher than the previous year and had attracted two pairs of owls to nest within easy reach of the Inuit settlement. They were ideally convenient for us, so we wasted no time before putting up hides near to both of them. The first nest, with a lovely background of rolling sedge meadows and shimmering sea ice, contained three newly-hatched chicks and two eggs. The youngsters were white and fluffy with oversize-looking heads clearly showing the curved beak and prominent yellow eyes, the trademark of their parents. They squeaked in anticipation of food when the mother returned to the nest, although most of the time she sat shading them from the surprisingly warm sun. We actually saw her panting from the heat on one particularly windless day when we were all, animals and humans alike, also suffering badly from a plague of mosquitoes!

Over the next few days, this nest gave us some superb shots of the mother owl, such as her outspread wings backlit against the evening sun as she returned to her brood. Martin also filmed her being cruelly harassed by a pair of long-tailed jaegers who dive-bombed her for minutes on end, while she was feeding herself on a nearby rock and also just sitting quietly on her nest. We wondered why the jaegers didn't try to steal the chicks on the rare moments they were left unguarded, but they seemed intent only on giving the adult owls a bad time.

Just before we had to leave Igloolik, the long hours of patient waiting in the hide paid off. In a single evening we managed twice to film not only the male delivering a lemming to the female on the nest, but also the female pulling it apart to feed delicately to her owlets. To further add to our delight, on the way back to the village Martin managed to creep close enough to film a male owl making a long, silent glide towards a patch of lush vegetation where, with powerful talons, he plucked up an unsuspecting lemming right in front of the camera.

The other nest was more advanced, containing five much larger owlets with lumpy, immature plumage. Their mottled grey colour and even the texture of their feathers matched almost perfectly the humps of lichen all around; a triumph of camouflage, necessary because both parents were now away from the nest out hunting in an effort to satisfy the appetites of their rapidly-growing brood, and no longer providing any protection. The nest area was surrounded by white feathers which made it easily visible, so as soon as they were strong enough the young owls wandered off in all directions, presumably to avoid predators. The first sight of these little grey bundles waddling around like clockwork toys we found highly amusing. Indeed, Martin was laughing so much that he had a job keeping the camera still enough to film, particularly when they ran straight towards him to snuggle under his lens for shelter and protection!

During the five days we were in Igloolik, all of these young owls spread out individually until they were somewhere within an area of about 100 metres in radius from the original nest site. We visited the location several

135

times, but found it more and more difficult to find the owls. They were virtually impossible to spot amongst the gravel and lichens, crouched down, absolutely still for much of the time, with even their giveaway yellow eyes half-closed. It made us wonder how on earth the parents found them when they had food to offer. The answer came purely by chance on our final afternoon in Igloolik.

I had left Martin and Jeremy in the hide at the original nest for a few last shots of the other female, while I paid a final visit to the area of our dispersed youngsters in the hope that, if lucky enough to spot one, I might take some stills. To my astonishment, everything was soon made very easy as, from several directions, what seemed to be hummocks of lichen were suddenly given little yellow legs and stubby, flapping wings, and were running towards me making intermittent high-pitched whistles. It being a chilly day, I was dressed in my white Arctic anorak and quickly realised that these hungry youngsters must have mistaken me for a parent snowy owl.

Continuing the pretence, I crouched right down and copied their whistling noise, which made them run even faster. Then, as they got quite close, their large mouths alternated between a wide gape and a high-speed rattle like the sound of castanets — obviously a begging call. They showed absolutely no fear: on the contrary, as soon as they realised I had no food, three of them waddled casually off while the remaining pair merely snuggled under my anorak, closed their eyes, and went to sleep. After a few moments in that position, I noticed the real father swoop into view from behind a nearby ridge and, not wanting to disturb or even disappoint those enchanting owlets any further, I backed away and slipped quietly out of sight.

HUNTERS OF THE NORTH

On comparing notes later, we learnt that by midnight on 23 June 1984, Hugh, in East Greenland, had already arrived in Ørsted Dal and was starting to film the famous ledge-nesting barnacle geese, while at the same time Martin Saunders and I were thankfully nearing the end of an arduous 150-kilometre journey by skidoo and sledge over the sea ice to the north of Baffin Island in Canada.

For the past twelve hours we had been jolting our way from the small settlement of Arctic Bay, northwards up Admiralty Inlet and then eastwards along Lancaster Sound. So far, we had stopped only three times, once to eat something and brew up some tea and twice to manoeuvre the sledges and skidoos over wide cracks in the ice – the latter being achieved with great ingenuity by our guides, the local wildlife officer, Glen Williams, and Jonah Oyukuluk, a cheerful Inuk hunter from Arctic Bay.

Faced with these open channels, in one case about 20 metres wide, they had calmly pushed several pieces of floating ice together to form loose-looking bridges and then driven very quickly across before any of the component bits had sunk under the extra weight! Our final destination, now only about an hour away, was the so-called 'floe-edge', the constantly-shifting line where last winter's ice meets the already open ocean – in our case, the northern end of Baffin Bay.

Lakes of slush and melt-water lying on top of the ice made the last part of the journey more like boating than sledging. The grey overcast sky added to the general impression of damp and cold, so that the thought of pitching a tent out there was far from inviting. Then, at about 1 a.m., just as we drew up at the floe-edge itself, the sun emerged below the distant line of cloud and in that instant the sombre scene was transformed by golden light to one of magnificent splendour and profusion.

Close to the jagged ice-edge, as far as the eye could see, swam literally

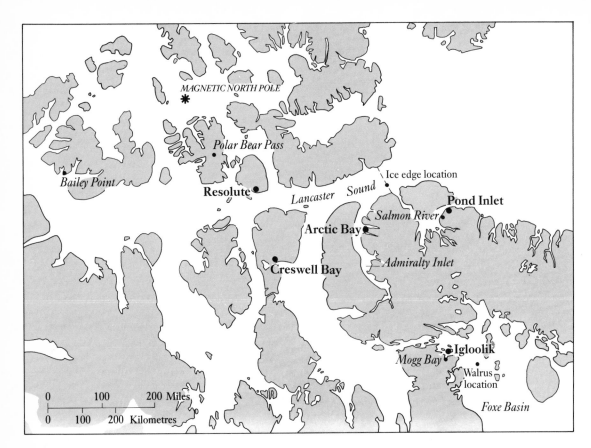

millions of thick-billed murres, some diving under the ice to feed at the same time as others bobbed back to the surface. Their constant high-pitched calls were overlaid by sounds of powerful breathing as groups of beluga (the white whale of the Arctic seas) and mottled grey narwhal swam in both directions a bit further out. A large, dark-looking bearded seal broke surface nearby, surveyed us with mournful-looking eyes for a minute or two and then dived out of sight again. A pod of twenty or so harp seals was dipping and turning away to our right, and several walrus gambolled in the water by the side of a large plate of flat ice which had recently broken off the ice-edge and was now gently floating out to sea.

For an hour or more, we stood there watching, captivated. The night was so calm that we could clearly hear the blowing and the strange whistling noises from whales several kilometres away. It was tempting to imagine that nearly all the animals in the Eastern Arctic had gathered in this one area to take advantage of the copious food supplies that we had seen and filmed a month ago under the ice, and which were now available here at the floe-edge. But we knew that *every* suitable ice-edge in the Arctic would probably be showing off the same spectacle of profusion, highlighting the immense productivity of these far northern seas.

In our various ways we were all delighted by what we could see. For Martin and myself it meant that the chances of filming beluga and narwhal

138

under the surface looked very promising. The water was clear and the animals were coming quite close without looking too nervous. For Glen Williams it appeared to be ample justification for suggesting both this particular location and the exact timing of the trip; and for Jonah Oyukuluk? Well, even though he knew that our primary concern was photography, he couldn't restrain his hunting instincts, and whenever a large male narwhal swam past in the clear water, showing off its beautiful ivory tusk, he danced around uttering joyous exclamations in Inuktutuk and throwing imaginary harpoons at it!

Having already been awake for nearly twenty hours, we were too tired that night to rig up all the gear for filming. The weather looked very settled, so we opted for pitching the tent about a kilometre back from the edge, getting a few hours' sleep and trusting that conditions would be just as good when we woke up.

At breakfast the sound of hundreds of whales blowing and diving only half a mile away added an air of expectancy to the meal. Fortunately it was still beautifully calm, so Martin fitted the film camera into the underwater housing and we made our way quickly to the ice-edge. On a previous occasion, Martin had attempted to film narwhal by diving with them, but they had been too nervous and never allowed him to get close enough. Now the plan was to lower only the camera into the water and work it from a lying-down position at the edge of the ice. The obvious disadvantage was going to be waiting in a static position for a whale to come into shot. Frankly we had no idea whether it would work or not. Glen had warned us that heavy footsteps meant 'polar bear' to the whales below and would quickly clear the spot of any animals, so we very quietly crept up to the edge and, while I took the strain on the safety rope, Martin eased forward on his knees to slide the camera into the water.

Almost immediately, a group of twelve or so beluga, which had been lying quite still about 300 metres out, began to swim slowly towards us. They were taking deep, regular breaths as they continued forwards, and Glen's hand signals made it quite clear that he expected them to dive under the floe-edge to feed. With any luck, on the course they were still heading, one or other of them might swim right past the camera.

The tension seemed unbearable as the whole group came nearer and nearer until, when about 20 metres away and still too far off to film, each took an extra large breath and dived. We thought that was the end of it, but fortunately they stayed in quite shallow water, two of them swimming almost directly into shot below Martin's camera. To add a final touch, three or four of the back markers, instead of immediately swimming under the ice, hung, gently finning, in the water ahead of us. They peered up inquisitively for a few moments, their pure white skin showing up beautifully in the filtered sunlight, and then gracefully, unhurriedly, followed the others below the ice.

As he switched off the camera and turned round, Martin's grin was nearly wide enough to push his ears off. But there was no time to bask in the delight of this early success for, very soon, other belugas, on return from their feeding session below the ice, were surfacing all around. As it was impossible to predict where or when they would appear, these shots were much more

*Above: seabirds
at the ice-edge*
Right: harp seals

140

Female narwhal

Below: beluga whales

difficult to achieve. Nevertheless, after only two hours we had already made some very good progress with nearly ten minutes of film 'in the can', mostly of belugas but also a distant underwater shot of a male narwhal, his impressive tusk showing up clearly. It was one of those marvellous moments in wildlife film-making when all the struggles and anxieties of budgets, research, production plans, travel arrangements and so on are totally forgotten in the euphoria of having successfully filmed a really unusual animal in a difficult location.

The technique of leaning over the edge of the ice and dipping only the front of the underwater camera housing, containing the lens, into the sea seemed to be working extremely well – at least it did not disturb the animals too much. However, it did mean that the viewfinder at the other end was out in the bright sunlight and consequently warmer than the rest of the camera. Condensation built up on the inside surface of the glass porthole, making it very difficult for Martin to see. The solution was to unscrew and remove the waterproof part of the viewfinder so that air could get in. It also helped Martin to get his eye close to the proper eyepiece in the normal way.

This made all the difference; he could now aim and focus with much greater certainty, but it was a calculated risk, as there was now a hole through which sea-water could potentially enter the camera. Glen promised to concentrate on holding the safety ropes taut, for he realised that our filming would be over if such an accident were allowed to happen.

Although many pods of both narwhal and beluga cruised continuously up and down the ice-edge, it was the belugas which seemed to be doing most of the feeding at that particular spot. Glen volunteered to skidoo along the edge to see if the narwhal were more active elsewhere, so we jolted Jonah Oyukuluk out of his hunting reverie to take over the job with the safety lines, and got back to filming.

Stupidly, we forgot to re-emphasise the importance of keeping the rear end of the camera housing out of the water and as Martin leaned on it slightly to film the next beluga going past, Jonah slackened the ropes in response and the whole unit slipped underwater. We reacted with lightning speed and in a few seconds had it out of the sea and tipped upside down. About a litre of salt-water came out, but knowing how ultra-sensitive the electronics of these cameras are to damp, we imagined it to be totally ruined and felt a large cloud of gloom block out the previous elation.

Using the sledge as a bench, Martin set about the tedious business of stripping the whole thing apart and meticulously drying everything off. Fortunately the weather was still totally calm and sunny; that much at least was a blessing. Inevitably, the narwhal also started to return in fair numbers, just when we were powerless to act. I tried to be philosophical, and just watch and enjoy that great natural spectacle.

With their mottled grey and white skin the narwhals didn't show up so clearly in the water as the all-white belugas. Nevertheless, they are impressive animals, particularly the adult males, which can weigh 1200 kilos and be up to five metres long, with a single pointed tusk adding a further two to three metres. That famous spiralled tusk is not a horn but an overgrown incisor tooth, usually on the left side of the upper jaw, although we did see two or three 'double-tuskers' which caused Jonah to leap up and down with even more animation than before. The function of the narwhal tusk is still a mystery, although it's thought likely to be a sign of dominance over rival males and possibly used for aggressive sparring when trying to obtain mates. We certainly had our best surface view of tusks when two males lifted them out of the water and moved them against each other in a crossed-swords position for several minutes at a time.

Both beluga and narwhal eat amphipods, arctic cod, squid and molluscs, and seemed to follow the same feeding pattern at the floe-edge. Groups of them cruised by in both directions, occasionally stopping to lie quite still 100 metres or so offshore. This was the time to keep an eye on them, for eventually they would turn to face the edge, start breathing more deeply and then slowly head in towards the ice. We soon learned to recognise when a narwhal was on its final breath because, unlike belugas, they lift up their tail flukes before finally diving under the ice. It was always a moment of mounting anticipation, for occasionally an individual would leave the 'fluke-up' very late, allowing us the best possible close-up view. Belugas came just as close now and again, but gave no prior indication of when they would make their final plunge.

Both species concentrate at the floe-edge where large plates of ice are constantly breaking off to reveal fresh feeding areas. Also, if any 'leads' open up inwards from the edge, the whales swim along them with a seemingly unstoppable urge to reach new locations. Inuit hunters are of course well aware of all these habits and, in the Eastern Arctic, come to the floe-edge or wait by leads in order to kill whales for food, the skin or 'muktuk' being specially prized as a vitamin source. The ivory narwhal tusk is also valuable, traditionally for making tools and carvings, but in modern times for selling to European dealers for a handsome profit.

It took Martin an hour and a half to dry out and reassemble the camera, after which, to our great relief, it seemed to work perfectly again. As luck would have it, we missed some potentially superb shots during the wait, but there was still a fair amount of feeding activity and by 8 p.m. we had twenty minutes of good film, including a rare shot of a large male narwhal swimming through frame looking like a sleek submarine fitted with a long nose probe!

The weather now looked changeable so, although we were tired, we had a short break back at the tent for supper and then returned to the edge to continue filming. There was something much larger and darker moving close to the ice, which we soon realised was the massive back of a bowhead whale. Having grown accustomed to smaller whales of four to five metres in length, a 20-metre bowhead looked like a monster by comparison, particularly when it lifted its enormous head, which takes up a third of the body length. We could clearly see then the creamy-coloured patch on the lower jaw and the long curved mouth full of baleen plates. A deep bass 'blow' and a lengthy intake of air gave an indication of the massive size of those lungs – and then, before we could get the camera ready, it dived.

Above: Pond Inlet in July

Right: Inuk mother and child

Far right: Inuk girl with wolf-lined parka

144

We could imagine the bowhead somewhere under us, mouth wide open to scoop in great quantities of water, containing perhaps thousands of swimming amphipods or krill. Every so often the mouth would be closing to force water out through the baleens. These plates of stiffly-fringed hair – the so-called whalebone – which hang from the upper jaw act like a sieve to trap the small crustaceans. The massive tongue then clears the prey into the gullet.

The high quality of their whalebone, along with the thickest blubber of any whale, and their slow speed, made the bowhead an easy and a highly-prized catch amongst American and European whalers in the eighteenth and nineteenth centuries. Inuit hunters have traditionally taken a few bowheads every year, both in the Eastern and Western Arctic, but that was small-scale cropping when compared to the massive, uncontrolled slaughter carried on by our greedy forefathers which, by early this century, had all but wiped the species out of existence.

After twenty minutes underwater, our gentle giant surfaced again nearby and we felt it a great privilege to be observing so closely one of perhaps only a hundred bowheads left in the Eastern Arctic. (The population on the Western Pacific side was not so thoroughly exploited and is thought to number 2–3000 animals still.) It was a serene evening, with plenty of other whales about, but they all seemed to be basking offshore instead of feeding, so we packed up just after midnight with a nasty-looking cloud bank rolling in from the east. I went to sleep fearing that after such a promising start we were going to be foiled by a change in the weather. My diary for the following day confirms my pessimism.

'Woke on 25 June to howling N.E. gale and wet snow. New crack opened up 50 metres in front of the tent. We went out to floe-edge, but waves now crashing over the top and the ice for 200 metres back heaving and breaking in the swell. Cracks open and close sending spurts of water into the air and we have to choose the right moment to jump between floes. A wild and impressive sight, but unwelcome. Seems alarmingly exposed on this 60-centimetre-thick ice, 25 kilometres from the nearest solid land, but Glen and Jonah say there is no danger while the wind is blowing towards the edge, keeping the broken ice floes packed together. If the wind drops or changes direction we must move *very* fast they say!

'In the meantime, we sat it out in the tent and by 2 p.m. it was blowing harder than ever. The swell was obviously increasing as a new crack appeared right in front of the tent door – a definite indication that it was time to move. We hurriedly packed up camp and loaded the sledges, but Glen's skidoo wouldn't start. Jonah and Glen seemed very calm as we tried to find what was wrong, but it was difficult to share their feeling, for by then the ice all around us was heaving up and down as each line of swell ran underneath. Luckily, when Glen removed a lump of snow from inside the carburettor, the skidoo started and we were soon heading to a new spot about 10 kilometres away, where the ice was miserably wet and slushy but at least felt *solid*.'

For the next day and a half we were confined to the tent while a blizzard raged outside. We slept a lot, talked a lot and ate – and the food we ate on that trip taught us much about the local diet. Glen Williams had promised to provide the food, which meant taking the usual supplies of an Inuit hunting party – tea bags and 'pilot' biscuits (a sort of thick cream cracker). A lump of frozen caribou meat was added as a concession to safety, but rifles and a harpoon would provide the rest. 'When you go out on the land you live off it; no point in weighing yourself down with tins of baked beans,' he said!

At our very first real break during the journey out to the floe-edge we had watched Jonah Oyukuluk and Glen expertly skin a freshly-shot ringed seal, before slicing off bits to eat, particularly from the liver, which when warm and raw is considered a supreme delicacy. When they asked us to try some it was doubtless intended to test our reaction early on, but although neither of us had eaten fresh, uncooked meat before we knew that any initial feelings of revulsion were far more cultural than rational and so, after a slight hesitation, we tucked in and enjoyed it.

The very name 'Eskimo' is a slightly contemptuous American Indian one meaning 'eaters of raw meat', which is partly why modern Eskimos prefer to be called 'Inuit' – 'the people'. But without raw meat, the Inuit would never have survived. In the Arctic it is the *only* source of all essential vitamins during most of the year. If the majority of the leaders of European expeditions to the Arctic had not been so blinkered in their outlook, they would have realised this simple truth and, instead of condemning Eskimos as 'animals' for eating uncooked meat, might have copied the habit and as a result saved the lives of the thousands of men who died of scurvy. Certainly during our own expedition to the floe-edge, Martin and I had little chance of suffering such deficiencies. By the finish of the trip, Jonah and Glen had introduced us to cooked and uncooked seal meat, blubber, thick-billed murre, eider duck, char and – most delicious and vitamin-rich of all – raw whale skin, the famous 'mukluk'.

I am very aware that writing about such things will cause some readers to shut this book in disgust. My own feelings about hunting are somewhat ambivalent. Having not been brought up to it I don't enjoy the 'sport' of killing animals. On the other hand, I can get equally excited when stalking them for photography, which I'm sure satisfies, for me at least, those very same hunting instincts.

Waste, however, does sicken me, so I was glad that Glen and Jonah only killed what we needed. Out there on the ice, surrounded by a multitude of animals, taking the odd one didn't seem out of place. Such thoughts led to talk about the dangers of having double standards and, as an illustration, Glen told us how his Inuk wife, on their first visit to a southern farm, was horrified to learn that we actually *raise* animals in captivity just to kill them.

Waste doesn't form any part of a traditional Inuit attitude to hunting either, although nowadays the older men complain that some of the young-sters, lacking the basic skills and being too impetuous with their high-powered rifles and skidoos, at times wound far too many animals, which then escape and die for no good purpose. Indeed, there was so much concern that narwhal were being overhunted, mainly because of the high value of their tusk, that in 1977 the species was protected by a quota system. In 1983, the total Canadian quota was 542 narwhal per year, distributed throughout twenty-one Arctic

Ringed seal

*Timothy Idlout
hauls in a
ringed seal*

148

Above and left: the Idlout family fish for char and prepare it for drying

149

communities, with Arctic Bay and Pond Inlet having the highest quotas at 100 each. Belugas are not protected by a quota, but are more plentiful than narwhal and, having no ivory tusk, are not liable to the same temptations of killing them merely for an easy profit. Nevertheless, wildlife officers and biologists monitor the populations of all the Arctic whales most carefully in the hope of guaranteeing their conservation for the future.

On the afternoon of 26 June, the storm eventually died down and we returned to the floe-edge to find that all the loose plates of ice had now floated off towards Greenland, leaving a new edge running right in front of our former tent position. We needn't have moved after all – although only a fool would have stayed. There was a frustrating twenty-four-hour wait before the whales came back in any number, but eventually we were able to complete our sequences, including some particularly fine shots of beluga mothers with their small grey calves. Then, on another perfect calm evening, Glen and Jonah went several kilometres further along the edge to try and harpoon the one narwhal which would complete their yearly quota, while Martin and I settled down for a last chance of underwater footage.

Suddenly, large numbers of beluga were swimming past us very close and fast, so much so that their wash broke over the ice-edge making us quite wet. They must have panicked at the moment when Jonah shot his narwhal: an unfortunate reaction to witness, but one which, by chance, gave us some of the best close-up footage of the trip. In discussion later, we all concluded that it was the long-term effects of just such violently-disturbed reactions to noise which were the major worry if proposals for all-year-round shipping in the Arctic went ahead. Giant ice-breaking tankers crashing through two-metre-thick ice would surely make far more noise than one shot and would set up a panic several kilometres away. The sobering thought that the yet unspoilt peace of this floe-edge and its animals might be permanently shattered in the future perhaps increased our reticence to leave on such a beautiful evening, but depart we did, and were back in Resolute by 29 June.

Waiting for us in Resolute were the three extra people needed to turn Martin and myself from a compact, wildlife-only unit into a full synchronous-sound film crew. They were Terry Woolf, a Canadian sound recordist from Yellowknife, Jeremy Humphries, camera assistant from BBC Bristol, and Judy Copeland, our long-suffering production assistant for the project, who had already done much work behind the scenes for all the filming trips, but until now hadn't been to the Arctic herself.

Our purpose was to film various sequences about human involvement with Arctic wildlife, most notably an unusual Inuit family still living off the land in a remote out-camp on Somerset Island. But before going there we took the opportunity to visit and film the proposed location of Canada's first Arctic National Wildlife Area – Polar Bear Pass on Bathurst Island. By good fortune, Stewart MacDonald, the biologist from the National Museum of Natural Sciences in Ottawa, who has campaigned long and hard for just such areas, was in Resolute and able to fly there with us.

150   Stewart is one of the wisest and most experienced of Arctic biologists. He

it was who invented the often-used phrase 'Arctic Oasis' in first describing
Polar Bear Pass. Viewing it from near the huts of the field station set up by
Stewart and his team in 1968 we could see quite clearly what he meant. The
surrounding highlands, like most of Bathurst Island, were quite barren: high
windswept ridges, too dry and rocky to support any vegetation, resembled a
genuine cold Arctic desert. In total contrast, the vast lowland area of Polar
Bear Pass is scattered with thousands of shimmering ponds and flushed green
by the extensive meadows of moss and sedge. 'Oasis' certainly seemed an
appropriate description.

Since the research station was established, scientists have identified no
less than sixty species of bird and nine species of mammal that use the oasis,
and that includes large herds of musk oxen, a pack of rare High Arctic white
wolves, and the polar bears that often wander through in the summer and give
the place its name. Nevertheless, Stewart shares with many others the opinion
that Arctic biological research has only just begun and while we wandered
around appreciating the beauty of the area he shared his thoughts:

'Today, polar regions are no longer remote. Faced with man's technological onslaught, the most distant and inhospitable environments become completely accessible and here in the north important ecosystems risk the familiar
threat of alteration or obliteration. I really believe it is urgent that the most
important habitats are protected. Also, we have to understand more about the
subtle interrelationships of life on the Arctic lands and in the polar seas while
they are still largely unspoiled. More funds are desperately needed for long-
term research. I often wonder,' he concluded, 'whether in the next century we
will be judged by our apathy, by our avarice or by our wisdom in planning the
future of the Arctic.' It would be good to imagine that, for a change, the last
option becomes reality.

Back in Resolute we filmed Buster Welch at work on some ice experi-
ments with his local trainee, Sam Idlout. We learnt that Sam was a son of the
same Idlout family that we were about to visit on Somerset Island, and that he
had recently opted to leave their remote haven and further his career in
Resolute, along with some of his brothers and sisters. Although this was now
his choice, he admitted that he *did* miss the freedom of the hunting life and the
peaceful setting of the family outpost camp of Creswell Bay on Somerset
Island. Seeing it for ourselves on a calm, sunlit evening, twenty-four hours
later, we could understand how he felt.

The family tents (they use wooden huts in winter) were set along the curve
of the shore overlooking Creswell Bay. It being only the beginning of July, the
sea ice was still solid except for a patch of open water near the mouth of a wide
river, where char were said to be prolific. Large bones were scattered along the
beach as witness to the beluga whales which regularly visit the bay when the
ice clears and whose meat and blubber have formed an important part of the
Idlouts' annual bounty for as long as anyone can remember. Birds, seals,
caribou, musk oxen, polar bears, fox and arctic hares are also on the list of
animals available to the family close by, which, together with eggs and berries,
are enough for total self-sufficiency both in food and clothing. Nowadays,

Right: the canoe journey to the walrus and the camp where the air was filled with mosquitoes

Below: walrus on the ice floe

*Flowers by
Salmon River*

*Snow goose nest
near the river*

Snow goose chicks

153

more char are caught than needed and the excess sold in Resolute to pay for skidoos, ammunition, fuel and so on. They also sell puppies from their husky team and occasionally make traditional Inuit clothes to order. Otherwise, life follows much the same pattern as in the past.

Timothy Idlout and his wife Nanga are about seventy years old – still seemingly fit and active and both with a lovely sense of humour. Neither of them speaks English, although all their children do, having been sent away to school. They are not against using modern aids like radio and transport to make life easier and more comfortable, but Timothy did tell us that he was not happy with people living in settlements like Resolute. He hears about alcohol and youngsters causing trouble and feels that if everyone were still in small outposts like Creswell Bay there would not be any of those problems. If his own children and grandchildren are anything to go by he certainly has a point. They are a delightful family and we much enjoyed our stay with them.

Timothy is obviously very matter-of-fact about killing the animals, which at the same time he greatly respects, but he will not tolerate waste. His eldest son, Simon, told us of his father's anger if any animal was killed when it wasn't really needed, and one of our best film sequences illustrates how the old man's preference for traditional hunting methods can also avoid waste.

We had gone out to film a day's seal hunting on the ice. Simon was keen to show us how he could creep up and shoot ringed seals as they lay basking by their breathing holes. But with numerous missed shots, the seals were merely frightened and quickly disappeared and his father suggested showing us a more efficient method if we had the time and patience to spare.

Timothy then set up near to a large breathing hole with his home-crafted harpoon attached to a length of bearded seal rope. He signalled to us to go a little way back and wait quietly while he crouched on his haunches, perfectly still, staring at the round patch of water. We felt that he could probably wait like that all day if necessary, but just as we were getting fidgety he sprang into action. The harpoon was thrown into the water and suddenly he was battling to haul a large seal out on to the ice. He is not a large man, but must be immensely tough because he managed to pull out the struggling seal on his own while we were filming and unable to help.

Back at camp, the seal skin was prepared by the ladies to dry and most of the meat cut up to feed to the huskies, all of which had started an incredible chorus of yowls from the moment they had seen us appear round the point. When the cacophony died down, we filmed Nanga and an older daughter Martha using their half-moon-shaped 'ulu' knives deftly to fillet the superb pink flesh of arctic char in preparation for the drying racks which at this time of year decorated the shoreline.

On our last evening at Creswell Bay, we joined the whole family as they took advantage of a large midnight run of char near the river mouth. Jigging through holes in the ice with pieces of musk ox wool on the end of a line, the fish are tempted to swim close and are then captured using traditional pronged spears called kakiwaks. Within two hours of golden midnight sun, accom-panied by much leg-pulling and laughter, at least 200 plump fish lay out on the ice, most weighing no less than five kilos. The Arctic can be a harsh place for man to live, but occasionally reveals her bounty.

On 5 July, while Terry and Judy flew southwards again, Martin, Jeremy and I headed east for the settlement of Pond Inlet situated on the north-eastern tip of Baffin Island. Scenically it's one of the finest of all the settlements, with superb views over the inlet to the mountains and glaciers of Bylot Island. Our visit was timed to coincide with the supposed date when the eggs of the snow geese would hatch. They nest in fair numbers a little way up the coast from Pond Inlet near the Salmon River, and in a normal year there should be the maximum number of goslings emerging between 8 and 11 July.

On the 7th we set up hides near two beautifully-located nests, and for the next few days we kept watch while the weather remained perfect. Our camp-site was spectacular and the mosquitoes almost unbearable! Then, during a sixteen-hour vigil on the 9th, our first nest hatched and the goslings staggered off with their parents to the nearest pond, enabling us to capture the event on film before the second nest put on a similar performance. We struck camp on the 11th just as the weather broke and by early on 12 July were on our way further south to Igloolik. If nature allowed all sequences to be as perfectly scheduled, we would hardly need to spend any time away from our homes!

We had exactly a week left to work in Igloolik and, apart from filming the Arctic flowers – which we did whenever the opportunity arose – we planned to join the famous walrus hunters of Igloolik as they went by boat amongst the ice floes of Foxe Basin. Nature now decided that she had been benevolent enough at Pond Inlet and provided instead such a variety of weather that sensible planning was made impossible. We kept receiving messages that conditions looked good for the hunt and would break off our snowy owl filming to make the bumpy two-hour journey to the hunters' camp on the far end of the island.

Inevitably a wind would spring up or a fog roll in and we would either be forced to go back to Igloolik or sleep at the camp in our tent. Eventually, on 19 July, the weather set fine, the camp burst into a frenzy of activity and by 2 p.m. we had everything loaded into the seven-metre freighter canoe belonging to Mark, the senior hunter, and were ready to depart.

Once we were through the jumble of floating ice close to the shore, there lay a vast stretch of fairly calm sea which Mark expected to be open for all of the 50 kilometres which he announced we would need to travel to find walrus. The outboard motor looked fairly new and reliable, but we couldn't help noticing that in the canoe there were no buoyancy compartments, no life jackets or flares, nor any kind of compass. I don't think any of us had realised how far out into Foxe Basin – notorious for sudden storms – we would be heading. While we were pondering these doubts, Mark's eldest son turned round from the bows, grinned broadly at us and said, 'Middle of nowhere, eh?' which seemed to sum the situation up perfectly!

After two hours' travel with no guiding landmarks and no technological aids, the navigation required to find the three other canoes which had left earlier seemed nothing short of miraculous. But find them Mark did, amongst a vast area of gathered ice floes where the hunters had already pinpointed a large herd of adult male walrus. As the whole flotilla of canoes glided gently towards the sizeable floe on which those massive animals were basking, Martin started filming. All the hunters knew that we wanted shots of undisturbed walrus because they had refused adamantly to allow us to film the hunt itself, but they still couldn't hold back and in no time at all bullets were flying. Within a few minutes, five great beasts lay dead, which was not a pretty sight and we were glad to be heading off on our own as the butchery process began. There is a strict quota system for the number of walrus killed each year and as we knew that five were all that remained of that year's quota we were at least encouraged by the control shown by the hunters. In that situation they could easily have slaughtered all twenty animals.

Away from the scene of carnage we found a stunning seascape of floating ice pans where the water mirrored the mackerel sky in such complete calm that it seemed difficult to tell which way up we were travelling! We were able to get close to several nice groups of walrus, including large families with young and massive adult males in twos and threes, all of them spending most of the time basking on ice floes, but some swimming and playing in the water.

Within a few hours we had all the film we needed and rejoined the hunters, who by then were in the final stages of bundling up the walrus meat into skin parcels of a most ingenious traditional pattern. The men were very cheerful but exhausted, and the journey back to Igloolik with the heavily-laden canoes was much slower. It gave us time, however, to talk to the hunters about their attitudes to wildlife and for them to voice a very strong criticism of the European ban on seal skins. They made the point that the slaughter of baby harp seals for their silver fur off Newfoundland was by white Canadian hunters and not the Inuit, and said they felt as angry as Greenpeace about the cruelty and the wasted meat left lying on the ice after the skins had been taken. But why had Europeans linked the Inuit with the harp seal pups and ruined the market for *all* seal skins? They vehemently pointed out that hunting adult ringed seals was much more skilled. It was carried out mainly for the meat but the spare skins provided a welcome extra income. Now, they suggested, the economics of many Inuit communities in Canada and Greenland were in ruins and more and more hunters were having to turn to the ignominy of welfare payments to support their families.

The truth of complex arguments such as these is always difficult to tease out, but these proud and fiercely traditional men of Igloolik did seem to have a strong case against over-reaction by the international conservation lobby in a situation where the facts might not have been fully appreciated. Certainly there was plenty to think about as we glided through the shore ice and back to camp. The midnight sun lingered above the horizon and arctic terns dipped for fish in a flame-coloured mirror of sea.

OF BEARS AND BIRDS

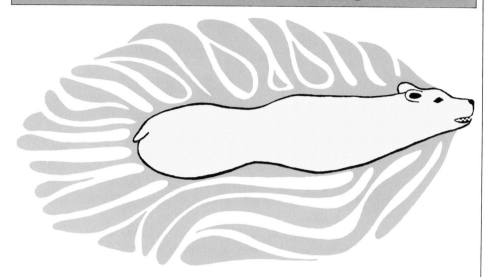

The view from our encampment on the narrow top of Caswall Tower was spectacular by any standards. We were perched 240 metres up on the edge of a narrow limestone block, which to the east and south fell jagged and almost sheer to the ice of Radstock Bay. On the other side of the flat summit platform, towards the west and north, the cliffs were eroded and tumbled into a series of steep scree slopes to the raised beach of grey stone below. That whole area of Devon Island in Canada's High Arctic was a monument to the power of erosion by wind and ice, with further great humps and cliffs of rock, very similar to Caswall Tower, left stranded, majestic, in an otherwise demolished landscape.

The date was 12 July 1983 and we had just pitched our sleeping tents near to the small wooden cabin that was erected several years ago by Ian Stirling's research group as an observation post for polar bear studies. Ian had generously allowed Hugh and myself to join him and his team while they continued observing the behaviour of polar bears. Our plan was obviously to film any bear activity we could, but in particular the stalk and capture of a seal – as yet, we believed, unfilmed.

All the scientific observations are made through telescopes set up to overlook the ice of Radstock Bay. The advantage is that even if the bears come very near to Caswall Tower their behaviour is never affected by human interference. It is simply too high up for them to see or smell their human watchers. From that supreme viewpoint, bears can be spotted 11 kilometres away, walking round Wallace Point and into the Bay from Lancaster Sound. In the other direction, to the north, it is possible on a clear day to see the 22 kilometres to the far end of the Bay, although 16 kilometres is about the maximum range of the telescopes to spot bears. Immediately opposite the hut, a four-metre-wide crack stretched five kilometres across the ice to Patrol Point and in its clear water hundreds of tysties (black guillemots) dive for food.

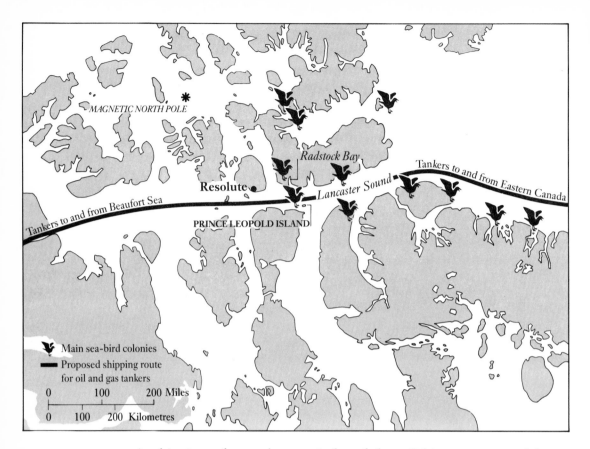

Main sea-bird colonies
Proposed shipping route
for oil and gas tankers

0   100   200 Miles

0   100   200 Kilometres

At this time of year the remainder of the solid ice was covered by an attractive but completely random pattern of firm snow interspersed with pools of light-blue melt-water. The idea was to keep an eye on the bears from the top of Caswall Tower so that when it seemed that they were heading in the right direction we could run down the scree to a camera position by the edge of the ice and film them from much closer. That at least was the theory; in practice we would need a little luck.

During the next few days we certainly had good fortune with the weather. It was even hot enough to sunbathe when the wind wasn't blowing. On the other hand, bears were nowhere to be seen. Indeed we all scanned for three whole days on a twenty-four-hour shift basis before the first one was spotted, about 12 kilometres off and heading our way between Waldegrave Bluff and Wallace Point. We thought that it being Hugh's birthday, 14 July, the sighting might be a good omen. But as we celebrated with a large tot of whisky and a birthday cake, the bear changed direction and headed back out of the Bay!

Another thirty-six hours followed without any bears in sight. Ian and the others admitted that in the eleven years they had been going to Radstock Bay it had never been that empty. To relieve our frustration, Hugh and I had a game of cricket on the surprisingly smooth gravel surface on top of the 'Tower': the most northerly game ever, we wondered? It lasted only until a turning ball from Hugh beat the bat and carried on over the cliff edge.

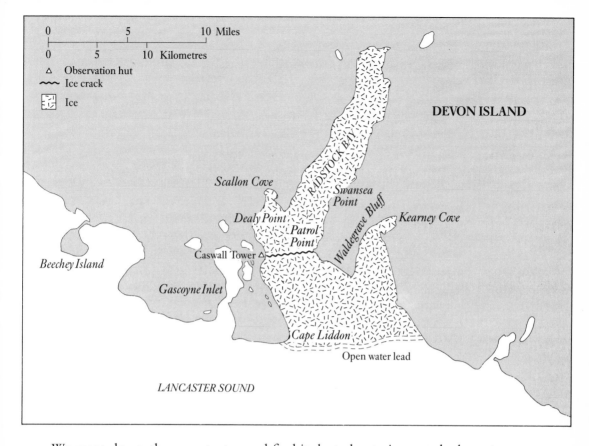

The map shows features including: DEVON ISLAND, RADSTOCK BAY, Scallon Cove, Swansea Point, Kearney Cove, Dealy Point, Patrol Point, Waldegrave Bluff, Caswall Tower △, Beechey Island, Gascoyne Inlet, Cape Liddon, Open water lead, LANCASTER SOUND.

Legend:
0 — 5 — 10 Miles
0 — 5 — 10 Kilometres
△ Observation hut
〜〜 Ice crack
Ice

We went down the scree to try and find it, but also to inspect the large shoreline rock from which we would film bears if we ever had the chance. Thinking that a dead seal which we found lying on the ice might attract a bear to come closer, we dragged it to a carefully-selected position in front of the rock at a distance of about 35 metres away, and looked forward to some results. The top of the rock gave us a small platform about six metres above the ice and a sense of security – quite possibly false, we soon realised, when Ian told us how he had once seen a large adult bear leap that height on to an iceberg!

At last, on the 16th and 17th, activity began to increase. On one day, a mother with two cubs of the year, or coys as they're known, walked to within 11 kilometres before turning away, and on the next, a mother with two yearling cubs came as close as five kilometres before veering off to the south-west. The antics displayed for our telescopes by the yearlings would have made superb film. It was tantalising that they didn't come closer, particularly as we saw one of them creep up and dive headlong into a pool containing two ringed seals. After a lot of thrashing around in the water, to everyone's amazement the cub dragged a small seal out on to the ice. At this age they don't usually succeed, so perhaps we had witnessed that young bear's very first successful solo hunt. Whatever the case, we would certainly have liked to film it.

159

*The camp at
Caswall Tower*

*Two yearlings
tucking into
seal*

*Below: bear
hunting seal*

Gradually, over the next two days, the number of bears within telescope range increased, and although for the moment none came near enough to film, we saw and learnt a good deal about their behaviour. With Ian, Dennis and Wendy we couldn't have wished for more knowledgeable guidance on the subject, and they were able to point out the different ways in which polar bears hunt ringed seals at this time of year. As we watched various bears in action through the telescope, Ian explained that the most common method is the 'still' hunt, where a bear waits motionless, usually lying down, by a suitable hole in the ice in the hope of grabbing a seal as it comes up to breathe. When bears change position they use a minimum of movement, because the slightest sound is transmitted through the ice to the water, and seals will not normally use a breathing hole if they hear any noise on the surface. But a bear's most dramatic method of hunting to watch is the stalk of a seal basking out on the ice. Sometimes the bear will lower its head and creep forward in a semi-crouched position, using any rough ice for cover. At other times, a bear will slip into the water and half swim, half crawl, through the interconnected pools and channels that interlace the surface of the sea ice in summer on what is called an 'aquatic stalk' and seems to be generally more successful.

The other style of aquatic hunting involves the bear actually swimming under the ice between holes, surfacing to breathe and look about, and diving again. Bears often have such marvellous control that they can surface, breathe, raise their heads slightly to look, and submerge without making a ripple on the water. From the data so far collected, it seemed that 'still hunts' are the most used and the most likely to be successful. Ian went on to tell us how surprised people were to hear that polar bear cubs in the High Arctic stay with their mothers until they are about two and a half years old. Coys seem to follow their mothers closely but not do any hunting as such. Indeed, they often ruin a stalk by getting overexcited at the wrong moment and warning the seal to escape down its hole. Yearling cubs also stay close behind their mothers, watching every movement and imitating it. If the female stops to 'still hunt', these younger cubs will also take up a 'still hunt' at more or less the position they were in when their mother stopped. From many hundreds of hours' observation it appeared that coys and yearling cubs are not yet effective hunters; they go through the motions, but rarely catch seals.

On the other hand, two-year-old cubs kill seals at a rate which begins to compare favourably with adult bears. They still move along in the same general direction as their mother, but often range one or two kilometres away, and choose their own sites to hunt. It appears that although cubs have learned to hunt fairly proficiently by the time they are two, they don't seem motivated to spend a large proportion of their time hunting, possibly because of the continued food supply being provided by the adult female.

We stopped our discussion for a moment to watch a mother with a couple of two-year-old cubs emerge from behind Waldegrave Bluff, followed at a distance of about two kilometres by a large male. The cubs weren't hunting, but gave a display of prolonged rough-and-tumble, splashing in and out of the pools – a delightful scene which we wished had been near enough to film.

'It's different in winter and spring,' Ian continued. 'We have noticed an unexpected lack of hunting by cubs of any age in those seasons, probably because until summer most seal breathing holes and birth lairs are buried under hard, compacted snow drifts. Even adult bears weighing up to 400 kilos need to pound on the snow several times with all their weight in order to break through into these lairs and breathing holes to catch a seal. It is likely that yearling and two-year-old cubs are simply not heavy enough to break through the snow in time to catch a seal before it escapes. All of these types of observations led us to the conclusion that if cubs are orphaned before they are fully weaned, they had far less chance of survival than those cubs able to stay with their mothers for the full two and a half years. We and other workers realised that maximum protection must be given to family groups, and Inuit hunters persuaded, if possible, to kill independent bears only.'

Ian was about to continue telling us how the polar bear hunting quota system came into being when Wendy drew our attention to a mother with a single yearling cub which had rounded Cape Liddon and was heading towards us along the edge of the ice. At the rate they were coming we would need to start down the cliff in an hour's time, so we scurried around putting the camera gear plus food and extra clothing into rucksacks, for we didn't know how long we would need to be away from camp.

Ian came with us as we set off fast downhill at 3 p.m. but we needed to concentrate hard because, with a 27-kilo pack, one slip could be nasty. Dennis broke his leg on the same descent two years ago. We were sweating like pigs by the time we got to the shore, but reached the top of the filming rock in twenty-five minutes and checked with Wendy on the walkie-talkie for a current position of the bears, as they were hidden from us by the curve of the cliff. She reported that they were still plodding our way and gave us an ETA of one hour's time. There was a strong and cold north wind sweeping along the cliff behind us, so we spent the spare time building a dry-stone wall around the top of our rock to afford some protection for the camera.

It was an impressive wall, a metre high at our backs by the time Wendy radioed to say that the mother and her cub should be in view at our position any moment. There was a mounting air of expectancy. Will they get our scent and veer away? Will they smell the seal carcass just 40 metres away on the ice and stalk that? – or us! Then suddenly there they were, cautiously approaching round the corner about 400 metres away. The mother bear smelt the air and turned further out on to the ice and the cub followed. After a few minutes she turned in our direction again, her black nose pointing high in the air to test the subtle odours that tell her something nearby might be edible. The cub copied her, always a few moments later. When they were about 200 metres away, the mother spotted our dead seal, but she must have thought it was basking out on the ice for she slipped noiselessly into a narrow channel of open water to start a full-scale aquatic hunt.

It was a breathtaking moment as she crept past us towards the seal, and Hugh's camera purred away quietly recording every move. Most of the time, only her ears and back were visible above the surface of the water, except

163

Ice bear stalks the frozen ocean

Mother and yearling cubs

Below: a loo with a view, and filming at Radstock Bay

Above: mothers with cubs

Right: the whiff of oxtail soup

Far right: bear on the ice at midnight

168

on, those arbitrary quotas have been adjusted, often upwards, to allow a sustained harvest of bears without damaging the population as a whole. The IUCN group met regularly to swap information on all the research that was being undertaken, such as the 'mark and recapture' work, and to draw up an agreement for international conservation and management of polar bears. This was signed in 1973 and came into effect in 1976, setting out guidelines not only about the conservation of bears but also their Arctic habitat.

We knew how long and hard Ian had worked together with the rest of the group for this unique achievement, so were not surprised when, with some feeling of passion, he told us, 'I think it's particularly significant that five nations from East and West bloc countries can come to an agreement on something as fundamental as the conservation of a species which is so symbolic of the Arctic and of all the other magnificent animals and ecological systems which exist around the polar basin. The fact that the agreement was renewed in 1981 to run in perpetuity has pretty well made it certain that polar bears are not and will not become threatened or endangered. In fact, they are probably now the best-managed of all the large Arctic mammals. But maybe what's even more important is that it might give a precedent to show that people and countries *can* get together to solve major conservation problems.'

Although the weather improved again over the next few days, the number of bears that came close enough to film dwindled disappointingly. This unexpected shortage meant that we had still only filmed the one mother and her yearling cub, but at least they had provided some really unusual scenes. Thankful to have achieved that much, we made plans to leave on 26 July, but Radstock Bay had one more event to show us. On our last night, hidden from view by a thick mist, the ice from the whole Bay south of the crack opposite the cabin moved out into Lancaster Sound and broke up, dramatically altering the view below within the space of a few hours. Where there had been ice before, there was now open sea, and many thousands of thick-billed murres were feeding along the new ice-edge. They had probably flown to Radstock Bay from Prince Leopold Island, visible 70 kilometres to the south, a spectacular seabird colony which we had already visited earlier in the month.

We had landed on the top of the eastern end of Prince Leopold Island on a beautiful calm and cloudless day amongst a prodigious carpet of lichens and purple saxifrage, presumably fertilised to that state of splendour by guano from the birds. Then, as we took our first look over the edge of the cliff, the noise and smell of thousands of murres, kittiwakes and fulmars battered the senses. At that time, in the second week of July, every suitable ledge and buttress was packed with nesting birds, an impressive sight, particularly against the background of broken ice and dark blue water 360 metres below. More than half a million pairs of birds nest on the cliffs, with murres and kittiwakes making up the bulk. It's a spectacle which emphasises how rich the supply of food available to these birds in Lancaster Sound must be, and has led to Prince Leopold Island being described as one of the ornithological wonders of the world. There is concern that such a massive concentration of birds might be very vulnerable to the effects of an oil-drilling accident or to disturbance from giant tankers which in the future may well crash their way through the ice nearby. Because of such risks, many wildlife biologists would like to see a total ban on development in the vicinity of Prince Leopold Island and the other major seabird colonies throughout the Eastern Arctic. But for the time being, tanker traffic and oil wells in Lancaster Sound are only ideas on paper, and the birds flourish in vast numbers as they have for thousands of years in the past.

Birds arrive at the island during May to start clamouring for nest sites on the ledges. Good positions get very crowded, so there is much jostling and fighting for each one. The peak of egg-laying is towards the end of June and early July. Certainly the majority of birds of all species were sitting on eggs in mid-July when we were there. Thick-billed murre pairs take it in turn to sit on the single egg, while their partner goes off to feed at a suitable ice-edge for up to twenty-four hours at a time. It is when they return to change duties that the precious egg is most vulnerable to predation by the ever-watchful glaucous gulls, who conveniently nest nearby. We filmed one of these largest of Arctic gulls stealing and swallowing a murre's egg whole without any difficulty at all. The owners might have layed again after eleven days or so, but deaths due to the onset of cold autumn weather are very high for chicks that hatch late. The Arctic might be bountiful in its supply of food, but the extreme shortness of the season does not usually forgive lateness.

The majority of murre chicks hatch at the end of July and early August and leave their nests to glide down to the sea before the end of that month. That, at least, is the timing for Prince Leopold Island and the other major bird colonies elsewhere in this part of the Eastern Arctic.

In Svalbard, however, the seabird nesting season is almost a month earlier; we had seen for ourselves the first birds arrive on the cliffs in early April. So, instead of the end of August, the chicks fledge at the end of July or in early August, a spectacular event at certain nest locations. Unfortunately, at that time of year everything happens at once in the Arctic, so Hugh and I couldn't manage to get to Svalbard ourselves and commissioned instead skilled wildlife cameraman Michael Richards to go there for us.

Consequently, on 25 July 1984, Michael was taken by helicopter, together with a Norwegian assistant, Erling Nordøy, to Bellsund, a large fjord 60 kilometres south of Longyearbyen, the tiny capital of Svalbard. The towering cliffs along the north side of Bellsund are the location for a massive nesting colony of guillemots. Between the base of the cliffs and the open water is a wide jumble of fallen rock and a gently-sloping flower-covered foreshore leading down to the beach. This layout means that the young guillemot chicks, when they are ready to leave the nest, instead of being able to drop straight into the sea as they would at Prince Leopold Island, have to fly across 800 metres of land before clearing the edge of the beach. As these young birds are unable to fly properly at first, they must launch themselves fearlessly off the cliff and attempt to glide into the sea on their stubby wings. Because they are not even very proficient at gliding, many land short and have to run the gauntlet of arctic foxes and glaucous gulls as they try to reach the sea on foot.

*Right and far
right: the sea-
bird cliffs at
Bellsund and
Leopold Island*

172

This was the sequence that Michael Richards had arrived to film, and the first fledglings were due to jump at any moment.

Michael and Erling settled themselves into a hut called Camp Millar, situated on the slope over which the birds would glide. Michael's diary captures the scene. 'The cliffs were magnificent, more open and vast than I'd imagined. The noise from the guillemots was like a distant swarm of bees, and the chattering from the little auks a constant background.' The little auks he mentions were nesting in their thousands on the scree slopes at the bottom of the cliffs. Here also was a fox den with cubs, nicely placed to plunder both the nesting auks and any guillemot chicks which arrived from above.

The weather in Spitsbergen in July and August is notoriously fickle and was to be Michael's most limiting factor, especially the low cloud which could hang over the mountains and cliffs and completely obscure the view. However, for a few days it remained fairly bright and on the evening of 26 July Michael wrote in his diary that the first birds had begun to leave the cliffs. 'Towards 10.30 p.m. there were a few young guillemots gliding with their parents. The youngsters looked unsteady in the air and about a third of the adults' size. I saw two crash-land on the ground, which left them with an exhausting long struggle to the sea. The parents go to the water and call – this is the sight and sound the gulls and foxes use as a cue for action.'

Michael also wanted to film other sequences – little auks, barnacle geese, arctic terns and so forth, but the main concern was the fledgling activity which we knew from research papers was concentrated in the evening and night-time. This was confirmed on the evening of the 27th as, after a day during which no more birds had left, he saw and filmed a few more guillemots jumping and gliding well with their parents on a wind which had sprung up during the afternoon. 'They all made the sea this time, six in half an hour at one point, although I saw the vixen bring one from the west to her cubs, who raced around with it as it was given. So obviously some chicks were not making it. Disappointingly, the weather turned misty and impossible for filming for the next two days, which made for some anxiety as the peak of fledgling activity was near and known to last for three or four days only.'

30 July also started cloudy but, as Michael recalls, 'The evening looked promising and the sun really came out. Some young guillemots began leaving the ledges and the vixen was quickly on to one which didn't make the sea. Then a second, half an hour later, crashed right below me, so I was able to film her carrying it to her cubs at the earth. I moved further down the slope in the hope of getting her chasing one. The guillemots had certainly started jumping in numbers now and I filmed another fox in lovely light, pursuing a chick which was running for the beach as fast as its weak little legs would take it; sadly, not fast enough to outmanoeuvre an arctic fox. I filmed many young guillemots gliding well, but landing untidily in the sea, where their parents gathered them into an ever-expanding raft of birds. At times the sky seemed to be full of parents and young swooping overhead. Although the majority seemed to reach the water, there were still so many for the foxes to chase that they hardly knew which way to go next!

'I got some interesting film, including a bird that crash-landed just before a fox ran up to grab it. The foxes killed as many as they could, sometimes trying to carry four or five in their mouths at one time before burying them in a cache for future use. The gulls tried to catch the guillemots on the wing, but grabbed more from the ground, often flying up with them in their beaks only to lose grip and drop them again. Even after such treatment, if the fledglings could escape recapture they might still make it to the sea. I filmed until well after midnight, when the sun went behind a bank of cloud, and then recorded some sound. It had been an amazing sight.'

Again, the weather turned nasty, a full gale to start with, so opportunities for Michael to take further film were very limited. He did manage a dangerous climb up on to the cliffs for some effective shots of the nesting ledges and the young birds exercising their wings in preparation for the big leap. He also took some nice shots of great rafts of guillemots gathered amongst the heaving swell, lit by a most dramatic stormy sky. They had continued leaving the cliffs in great numbers even through the nights of mist and drizzle, so that by 8 August, when he had to leave, the ledges above Camp Millar were beginning to fall silent and a feeling of autumn hung in the air.

When Hugh and I came to view the film Michael Richards had shot during those few days of dedicated hard work at Bellsund, we immediately realised that he had achieved a brilliant sequence of a most spectacular natural event and one which would be a high point in our first programme about the ecology of the Arctic Ocean.

MEADOWS OF THE MUSKOX

Looking down from the Twin Otter as we flew westwards from Resolute across the southern tip of Bathurst Island and then the great bulk of featureless land that forms Melville Island, it was difficult to imagine those dun-coloured stretches of dry, broken rock supporting any more life than the surface of the moon. Yet here we were on 11 August committed to the most expensive air charter of our entire project, supposedly heading towards one of those 'Arctic oases' – this one known as Bailey Point – where the polar desert turns green and animals graze in abundance. To believe it, from the evidence below, remained at that stage merely an act of faith.

Accompanying Hugh and myself on that journey was Anne Gunn, an experienced wildlife biologist working for the Northwest Territories' government. As one of the foremost specialists in the affairs of caribou and musk oxen, it was she who had suggested this venture in the first place. In 1979 she had visited Bailey Point, a smallish peninsula on the south coast of Melville Island, and been impressed by the high numbers of musk oxen there and the lushness of the vegetation compared to the extremely barren surroundings. When we had asked her advice about the best place to film the autumnal rutting behaviour of musk oxen, she had immediately suggested Bailey Point. It was relatively compact, totally undisturbed by hunting or development, scenically very attractive, and could offer Peary caribou, many bird species and arctic wolves as added possibilities for photography. So keen had she been to revisit Bailey Point herself that she had offered to come on the expedition as guide and adviser during her own leave, and only she knew exactly the sort of location we were all heading for.

Three hours later we were suddenly over land miraculously tinted green with small groups of musk oxen lying down or gently grazing. Bailey Point looked promising indeed as we flew up and down the peninsula for a recce before deciding to camp on the southernmost tip. From that spot we would be able to range east or west to find musk oxen, although we had seen two groups quite near to the place our pilot selected for landing.

Admiration for the strength of the Twin Otter was increased yet again as we touched down on what must have been the equivalent of a hard-baked ploughed field. The juddering was so violent that it seemed the whole aircraft would shake itself to bits at any moment. However, pilot and plane remained unconcerned as we lurched to a halt and started unloading the mountain of supplies which had filled every available space. Tents, radio, food, beds, camera equipment and stoves piled up on the ground, followed by three large Honda all-terrain motor trikes, together with drums of fuel for heating and transport. At this time of year, bad weather could make a return flight impossible for weeks on end, so we had come fully prepared for a long stay if necessary. But for the time being, as our link with civilisation took off and disappeared back towards Resolute, conditions were calm and sunny and ideal for setting up camp.

The site we had chosen to pitch the tents was on top of a dry ridge of clay about one kilometre away from the seashore. It afforded a marvellous view-point for spotting animals and was far enough away from the beach, we hoped, to lessen the chances of being surprised by wandering polar bears. In the bay immediately to the south of us the sea was still solidly frozen, the gleaming white of the ice contrasting sharply with the dark hills of Dundas Peninsula beyond. To each side of us the sparsely-vegetated clay ridges were interspersed with wide meadows of sedge and cotton grass, studded with shallow ponds. They looked green and lush and ideal places for musk oxen to graze. Behind us, stretching inland for about ten kilometres, were a series of dry rolling pastures leading to the escarpment of much higher barren hills that make up the island's interior.

In order to have a decent-sized retreat for cooking, eating and sitting in through the expected early autumn blizzards, we had borrowed a very large four-by-three-metre frame tent. This was roomy enough to take two camp beds for Hugh and myself, cooking equipment, chairs and a fair-sized oil heating stove, with a chimney pipe which went through an asbestos-lined hole at the rear. All very comfortable but, as Anne had rightly pointed out, if we needed to stay for several weeks there was little point in slumming it unneces-sarily! Firstly, however, we had to strive to assemble the tent's enormous tubular aluminium framework, which was designed a bit like a Chinese puzzle and took about as long to solve. Nevertheless, by 8 p.m., the main tent was finally up, together with a smaller one for Anne to sleep in, and another for the camera gear. Having also fetched a good supply of water from the closest lake, put up the radio aerial, made the first transmission to Polar Shelf and had supper, we were in good shape for an evening's filming.

The nearest herd of musk oxen were about two kilometres away to the west, down by the seashore. They hadn't been frightened off as far as we had expected when our plane landed, which we took to be an indication that at this time of year they might not be as nervous as when we had filmed them back in April. The totally calm, almost balmy evening was also in sharp contrast to the icy gale of that former occasion, although it was a useful reminder of the extremes of temperature which these Arctic animals have to cope with.

We drove along the beach on our Hondas to within half a kilometre of the herd. They showed only a slight disturbance, but we waited for them to settle as we wanted if possible all our film to show nicely-relaxed musk oxen. So many films we had seen previously had portrayed animals running around in fright or forming up in their customary defensive circles: spectacular but not a true impression of these normally docile beasts. We wanted spectacular foot-age – but only when caused naturally by males becoming aggressive with one another, rather than through anything we might do.

Indeed, the timing of our trip to Bailey Point was designed to coincide with the mid-August peak of musk ox mating behaviour. It is then that the females come into oestrus and are attractive to the dominant herd bull, a fully mature adult, who will try to mate with all the cows in his herd. He will have to work hard to stop any of the cows wandering away, but more particularly to ward off the attentions of younger, upstart bulls or other vagrant adults who might try to mate with his cows. Anne had told us about the fights that take place between rival bulls who will charge at each other from anything up to 60 metres apart, until meeting head-on with a resounding crash of thickened horn and skull. This ritual action might be repeated again and again, the noise echoing round the hillsides, until one or other runs away defeated. We knew such scenes, captured on film, would be spectacular and unusual, but just now the animals were calm, having settled back to their gentle grazing.

The low evening sun was producing such an attractive clear light for filming that as soon as the cows had their heads down Hugh began to creep forward along the beach towards them, hidden under the lee of a low bank. Anne and I had arranged to signal to him when he was opposite the musk oxen so that he could climb up the bank to gain a good viewpoint. There were seven cows in the herd, four of them with calves; two sub-adult bulls and a massive herd bull made up the remainder. Anne said that herds could vary in both size and composition of age and sex, but that the one we were looking at was about average. Young males may wander away from the herd of their birth at any time up to the six years it takes them to reach full adult weight. They will often form bull-only groups, from which in autumn they might split off again in order to challenge established herd bulls. What we would be on the lookout for were just such 'spare' mature males; following them should, in theory, lead us to some lively action.

For the moment, however, Hugh had reached a good position, so we gave him a signal to start his final stalk. Although he was probably within about 60 metres of the musk oxen none of them looked jumpy, so he had no doubt successfully found himself a good filming position without being noticed. Anne and I could merely wait for his return and in the meantime appreciate the surroundings.

The narrow shingle beach, backed by a low bank of clay or grass, was potentially quite dull to view. What elevated the scene above the ordinary was the sea ice. It seemed incongruous in a way – glistening white and blue against

Above: loading everything but the kitchen sink

Above right: our roomy tent at Bailey Point

Right: searching for musk oxen

181

the dry colours of a late-summer landscape. The wide stretch of sea in front of us, Liddon Gulf, was still packed solid with relatively flat ice. Along the shoreline, however, there was a wide band of clear water interspersed with stranded icebergs in a variety of sizes, many of them grotesquely shaped by continuous melting and refreezing. On one of the highest perched a group of lovely ivory gulls, and beside the smaller blocks lodged on the tide-line ran little groups of turnstone and sanderling, pecking away at crustacea amongst the litter of kelp. Every part of the scene was mirrored in the totally flat water, rippled only by an occasional drip from the corner of a melting iceberg.

The reverie was broken by a long, deep-throated roar which, if we hadn't just been looking at icebergs, I would certainly have passed as a large male lion, presuming the Arctic to be a dream. It was, however, the bull musk ox taking objection to Hugh, who by then (he told us later) had crept to within 30 metres and got some very useful close-ups. The impressive roaring continued until we saw Hugh emerge backwards from a gap in the bank. He was giving ground to the angered bull, who followed him for part of the way, pawing at the ground. When Hugh joined us again, Anne said how sensible he had been to retreat. Several biologists and photographers had been badly hurt or killed by enraged bulls during the rutting period, and we could imagine that, if one did take it into his head to charge, it would be little different to being hit head on by a speeding minibus! At 1 a.m., as the sun dipped below the hill, we returned safely to camp, very satisfied with such a promising start.

The following morning we set off eastwards in the hope of finding a herd of musk oxen with more than one bull in attendance. Our Honda three-wheel motor trikes very soon proved their worth. With a decent-sized luggage rack at the rear to hold camera gear, food, film stock, guns and so on, we could easily take what we required for a whole day out. The powerful engines and enormous soft-balloon tyres enabled us to travel over some very rough country much more quickly than we could have walked. Even so, continuous lolloping over the dry tufts and ridges of that wild landscape was very exhausting, so we quickly learnt to use the smooth shingle beach as our main rapid highway, branching off at 90 degrees for the slow, rough part when we wanted to get closer to musk oxen. Quite apart from being thoroughly practical, driving these machines was great fun – although each time we sped along the beach we were conscious that around any corner we might come face to face with a polar bear. But despite several tracks in the shingle we somehow, to our mutual benefit, avoided each other.

The first musk oxen we came across were in a very small group – only four females, one calf and a smallish-looking adult bull. Nevertheless, they were in a most attractive setting very near to the shoreline with a large iceberg in the background, so we took a few general introductory shots before moving inland towards a much larger herd we had spotted several kilometres away. After an extremely bumpy couple of hours we were in a good position between two separate herds – one up on the steep side of a small dry valley and the other, a larger group with twenty or so animals, peacefully grazing on a damp meadow of sedge.

Disappointingly, neither herd had any other bulls in attendance that had the slightest hope of challenging the massive herd bull. There were certainly several three- to four-year-old males which occasionally tried to show an interest in those cows obviously on heat, but when the patrolling herd bull saw what was going on he would start to advance, roaring in fury, and the smaller males would sensibly run for safety. We filmed some minor scuffles and some running around but, so far, this was not the dramatic spectacle we had been expecting. Somewhat worrying also was that, by the end of the day, we had covered perhaps 50 kilometres without seeing any solitary prime bulls wandering around looking for a herd to fight their way into. It was too early to be pessimistic but, back at camp, Anne agreed this situation was unusual. She could merely hope that with such a good choice of herds around it would only be a matter of time before we chanced upon some more exciting action.

Apart from a lack of prime bulls, what we had seen so far confirmed that for sheer numbers of musk oxen, regardless of sex and age, Bailey Point was certainly a superb location. We wondered if it was exceptional or whether elsewhere these fine animals were an endangered species. Anne told us that musk oxen in the Canadian Arctic certainly had been on the brink of extinction. During the eighteenth and nineteenth centuries, hunting increased very rapidly with the introduction of firearms to native hunters. Added to this, the demands of fur traders, overwintering whalers and European explorers, who wanted fresh meat to combat scurvy, saw the population of musk oxen decline inexorably until, in 1917, the Canadian Government passed regulations which prohibited virtually all hunting, fearing total extermination. That was the turning-point, for since then musk oxen have made a steady comeback and Arctic Canada now holds about 70% of the world population. With numbers of up to 18,000 on Banks Island, for instance, hunting has even been allowed again, although only on a strict quota system. 'I think the increasing populations of musk oxen are a striking testimony to the success of protective legislation,' Anne concluded.

The next day Anne went off on her own towards the west to check out the herds in that direction, while Hugh and I returned to the largest of yesterday's two groups. We spent several hours with them, eventually getting very close to the animals and managing to film all that we required by way of introductory shots. Certainly we now had material to illustrate how well adapted to the cold musk oxen are, with their short stocky legs and dense hair covering every single part of their bodies except for a small bare patch between the nostrils and the lips.

We also had film to show a range of pre-rut activity, particularly the herd bull pacing up and down testing the females for oestrus and keeping any younger upstart males away from those who were becoming receptive to mating. It was noticeable that whilst the cows and immature bulls could spend most of their time eating or chewing the cud, the poor old herd bull had to spend the majority of *his* waking hours advertising his grandeur and attending to sexual matters. So, while the others chewed steadily away, building up vital fat reserves to tide them over the approaching winter, prime bulls all around

Bailey Point were only able to grab the odd mouthful in moments of rare inactivity. Although we didn't know it at the time, this was a factor that was going to affect us as well as the bulls.

Behaviour died down to such a minimal level by afternoon that Hugh fell asleep with his head on a soft hummock of moss, leaving me on the lookout for any filmable action or wandering polar bears. He woke up two hours later to the sound of loud snoring, due partly perhaps to the heavy rifle lying across my chest! The herd had grazed themselves out of sight down a small valley, so we felt somewhat deflated and returned to camp.

Below: wildlife filming is not always exciting

An unexpected paradise

Below: sparse grazing for musk oxen

Anne returned some time after we had made the standard 7 p.m. radio schedule with Polar Shelf and was also not overjoyed with her day. Before telling us anything, she threatened to shoot her Honda trike; for about three hours at the farthest point of her journey it had apparently refused to start. Anne has little patience with mechanical aids which don't work and had stubbed her toe while trying to kick the trike into submission!

However, her more serious concern was that she had found some fine herds of musk oxen to the west but none had more than one prime bull, and two bands of females had no adult bull at all. Furthermore, she had started to examine carefully the many skulls that were lying around and found that significant numbers were the remains of prime bulls. She had not as yet looked at enough skulls to make a proper scientific judgement but felt sure that we were witnessing the effects of a massive winter die-off. As she explained to us, 'Weather is the dominating natural influence on musk ox populations. Very severe winters and springs affect not only the number of calves born but the number of adults which can make it through the summer. Normally a musk ox can paw through the snow to get to the vegetation, but this can be made very difficult by deep snowfalls or when the ground ices over from continuous thawing and refreezing. Malnutrition follows such conditions and animals start to die, especially those which haven't built up sufficient fat reserves the previous autumn to tide them over the period when food is scarce. Prime bulls can be particularly susceptible because if there are a lot of them around at this time of year the level of aggression can be very high while they battle over the females. Fighting and sexual activity leaves little time for feeding.'

If Anne's hunch was right, we were staring defeat in the face. However hard we looked we might not find a single prime bull that had any good reason to fight. With enough females on offer and no rival bulls worth speaking of, the rut, as an event, was as good as cancelled. Even so, we felt that Bailey Point was such a beautiful and unique location that, if it did fail us on the rut, at least other good things must come out of the visit. In that more optimistic frame of mind we headed directly inland next morning towards the hills to see if a change of country might improve our fortunes. We had in any case noticed two Peary caribou on the distant hillside which we wanted to film if we could get near enough. Peary caribou are the smallest sub-species of Canadian caribou and are found only on the High Arctic islands. They are very thinly scattered over a vast area, so it would be a piece of luck to be able to photograph them fairly near to camp.

From the coastal lowlands, the interior hills rise in a series of clay plateaux. These are dry and sparsely vegetated with fine grasses, mosses, arctic willow and dryas, all of which are on the musk ox's menu. Most of the musk oxen were at that time of year grazing down on the wet sedge meadows around the coastal lowlands, but in winter these exposed plateaux and ridges would collect less snow and probably become the preferred feeding areas. Certainly we began to find even more skeletal remains of musk oxen; many, Anne thought, being animals that had died only the winter or spring before. We took the opportunity to film her examining the skulls to show how, by

careful measurements and inspection of the horns and teeth, she could form a
good picture of the animal's age and sex before death. Some of the bones showed signs of having been gnawed by a carnivore larger than a fox, which conjured up tantalising images of a pack of pure white arctic wolves at work, their breath steaming in the clear frosty air. If we could only see and film such an increasingly rare scene, we would willingly have forgone the musk ox rut. But from the evidence building up of a massive die-off of prime bulls, it began to look more and more likely that any such fanciful choice was now firmly out of our reach. So, for the moment, we turned our attention instead towards the two Peary caribou, which were by then only about a kilometre away. We began to creep carefully forward although, as Bailey Point was too remote to be visited by Inuit hunters, we expected the caribou to be as unafraid as the musk oxen.

Surprisingly, when we had covered less than half the distance, they took fright and disappeared like pale ghosts into the shelter of a long valley. By the time we could get to a higher viewpoint they had drifted away some distance and were still trotting, so we thought it would be fruitless to go in pursuit. As we sat and watched them get smaller, Anne told us that as a sub-species Peary caribou were now in danger of extinction. In the High Arctic it's been estimated that their numbers have declined over the last fifteen years by about 80–90%, and the main cause is quite simply the weather.

As with musk oxen, deep or heavily crusted snow or a layer of ice over the ground can prevent Peary caribou from foraging and force them to move around, using up precious energy in a desperate search for food. They often cross the sea ice between islands, but during a very severe winter might not find anything better on the other side, so that by spring they are often just skin and bone. Then, during the brief summer – and a poor one can be as short as six weeks – they must feed enough not only to replenish any damaged tissue from the preceding winter but to build up new fat reserves to carry them through the next nine to ten months of winter. That's a tall order considering the sparse nature of the vegetation.

Anne emphasised that the knife-edge existence of these lovely and unique caribou meant that hunting and the effects of human disturbance in general would need to be very carefully monitored in the future if they were to survive. Perhaps remote Bailey Point might one day prove to be a permanent refuge for musk oxen and Peary caribou. From where we sat at that moment, with the rolling hills of thin grass tinged golden by an early frost, we sensed a strong reminder of another precious wilderness area – the Serengeti plains of East Africa. If a cheetah had crept from behind a hummock just then, we would not have been at all surprised.

Later that day we drove along the beach for about 20 kilometres to look at one of the larger herds of musk oxen that Anne had found the day before. Perhaps a stray bull had appeared and the rut was in full swing – a hope which not surprisingly went unrewarded. But there was some compensation in the sheer beauty of the scene: over twenty musk oxen peacefully grazed amongst the backlit seed heads of a cotton-grass meadow. To us it was an unexpected

Anne inspecting musk ox skull

Below: bog cotton and arctic fox

paradise that, reluctantly, we would have to leave earlier than expected, for without the dramatic musk ox rut we would shortly run out of worthwhile film subjects.

During the next morning's radio schedule we arranged for a Twin Otter to pick us up in two days' time – 17 August – and ferry us to Polar Bear Pass on Bathurst Island. This plan would hardly cost us any more flying hours as it was virtually on the way back to Resolute, but perhaps the musk oxen we knew to be there would include the essential spare bulls needed to foster some aggression. In the meantime, we would continue searching Bailey Point in order to achieve as much as we possibly could from the situation as we found it.

As expected, despite spending the two days before our departure covering several hundred kilometres on our Hondas and finding many fresh herds of musk oxen, none had any extra prime bulls. The hard winter had done its work thoroughly which, considering how settled and unusually pleasant the weather was at that moment, seemed cruel luck – both for ourselves and the musk oxen. However, we took advantage of the conditions to complete several sequences, including all the musk ox courtship and mating behaviour except for aggression. Waders were fattening up for the imminent journey south, brant geese, king eider and long-tailed ducks swam with their delightful young broods, and the plants were setting seed and turning colour as the first sharp frosts reminded us that in more average years there would already be snow on the ground.

Then, on the morning of 16 August, as if Bailey Point was trying to provide some compensation for other disappointments, we woke to a low, continuous roar and were able to film the majestic spectacle of the entire bay-full of sea ice breaking up and moving away at speed on the ebbing tide. The next morning, as we broke camp and tried with difficulty to fit everything back into the waiting aircraft, we noticed that the newly-opened water of Liddon Gulf had refrozen overnight. It seemed almost as if we had witnessed the end of spring and the start of winter all within the same twenty-four hours.

Despite it being a very interesting location, our three days at Polar Bear Pass were a great disappointment. The musk oxen we did eventually find were not only a long way from the base huts over some extremely rough terrain, but were also, yet again, without any fully adult spare bulls. Even the snowy owls let us down for although several pairs were flying around, none of them had nested, due probably to a lack of lemmings. Anne suggested that our best remaining option was to return to Resolute and from there go southwards by helicopter on daily filming expeditions to Prince of Wales Island. It would be an expensive risk, but a recent count had shown quite high numbers of musk oxen over there.

The predicted bad August weather came to Resolute the moment we arrived back, and during a frustrating week of hanging about only one day turned out to be flyable. On the grounds that it might offer our very last chance, and to enable the helicopter to fly more hours, I gave up my weight for extra fuel, leaving Anne to guide Hugh and the pilot to the likely musk ox locations. I spent a somewhat anxious day wondering how they were getting on, particularly as there was a nasty-looking bank of fog hanging over Barrow Strait which prevented any view of the islands beyond. However, at 6.30 p.m. the familiar throb of the returning helicopter brought me rushing out to greet two very worn-out-looking passengers. Long hours in a helicopter always make one feel dazed and uncommunicative for a while, so Hugh's simple phrase: 'We've cracked it, Mike!' was enough for me to know that they must have been successful.

Over supper, Hugh described how they had landed near to a group of musk oxen which, at long last, included a pair of large adult males preparing for battle. He had been able to film all the preliminary behaviour, such as walking up and down parallel to each other, roaring loudly and pawing at the ground. Then he had crept a little closer just in time to focus on them again as they turned and ran at each other from a good 50 metres apart. As their enormous bony heads had crashed together, the long hair hanging from their sides had swung back and forth like heavy curtains. Hugh's description was encouraging and it certainly seemed that at last we had filmed the vital sequence which had eluded us so frustratingly elsewhere.

CLASH OF THE CARIBOU

29 AUG 84

ATTN HUGH MILES, BBC NATURAL HISTORY UNIT, BRISTOL, ENGLAND
FROM JOHN ZIGARLICK, JR, ECHO BAY MINES LTD, EDMONTON, CANADA
RE: LUPIN MINE VISIT (YOUR LETTER DATED AUGUST 10TH)

YOUR TIMING FOR A VISIT APPEARS TO BE SEVERAL WEEKS LATE. THE PRIME COLOR CHANGE IN THE TUNDRA TOOK PLACE AROUND THE 22ND OF AUGUST.

WE ARE NOW INTO WHAT WE CALL THE 'BROWN' TIME AS FAR AS TUNDRA COLORS GO, AND ONE MAIN HERD OF CARIBOU MOVED THROUGH THE AREA 10 DAYS AGO. THERE IS PART OF ANOTHER HERD MOVING THROUGH NOW SO IT'S OUR OPINION YOU HAVE MISSED THE COLOR SEASON ON THE TUNDRA (WHICH BY SEPTEMBER 10TH WILL PROBABLY BE A LOT OF WHITE) AND UNLESS WE HAVE A LATE FALL, THE CARIBOU WILL ALL HAVE GONE BY THAT TIME.

SUGGEST YOU PLAN FOR NEXT YEAR ABOUT THE 25TH OF AUGUST.

REGARDS,
JOHN ZIGARLICK, JR
ECHO BAY EDM

This telex came as a shock, for our research had suggested that 10 September would be the ideal time to film the transition of the Arctic tundra from summer to winter. Postponing the trip for a year was not the answer, for by then the films would have to be complete. Advancing the trip was not possible, for I would be in North Africa working on another project until early September. Mike and I would just have to assume our research was correct and John Zigarlick had misinterpreted our requirements.

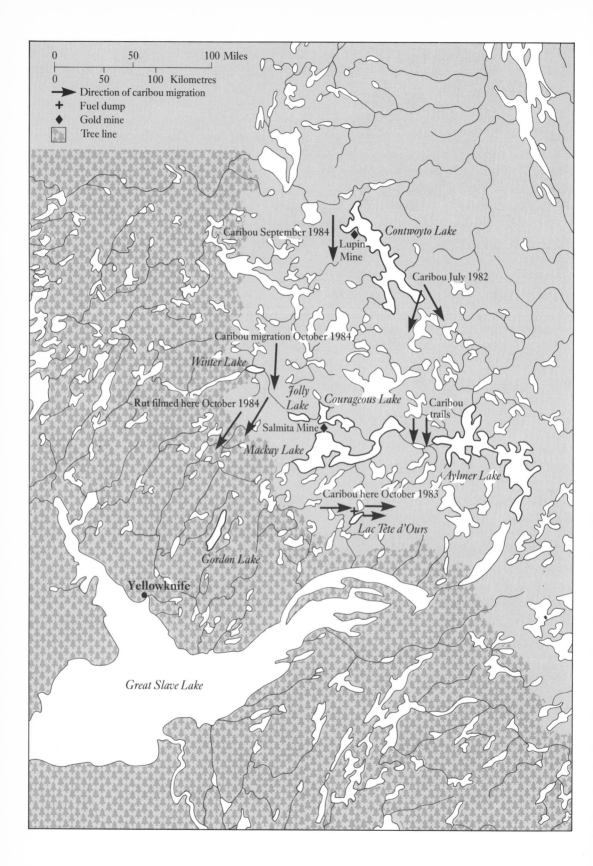

John is president of Echo Bay Mines in Canada, and his telex was a reply to my request to use the Lupin Mine as a base for filming. It is situated far out in the Barren Grounds of Canada, the most northerly mine in the Western hemisphere, and placed as it is on the western shore of Contwoyto Lake, it might be the ideal location to film the tail end of the caribou migration and the first snowfalls of the winter. We also wanted to film the glorious autumn colours, but were we too late? It was with some trepidation that I travelled from Edmonton to Contwoyto Lake in the mining company's jet.

On landing it was soon evident that my journey was not in vain. The tundra around the mine was indeed colourful, snow had not yet fallen, and a few caribou fed alongside the distant lake shore. Constantly alert to the fact that they might be the very last of the migrating hordes, and also anxious about the threat that at any moment the whole scene could be transformed by a blizzard and then stay white for the next nine months, I rushed out with the camera almost before the dust from the jet had settled.

It was Bill Mason, the distinguished Canadian film-maker, who believed that the intensity of an artist's response to a scene or a place will depend in some measure on how he got there. 'The faster we travel, the less we see. Perception is won by experience, we come to know our subject by living with it, and we must work hard for the knowledge that we render into artistic forms.' By these criteria we had certainly worked hard for our film in Svalbard in the spring, but with my transformation from home in Dorset to the heart of the Canadian tundra in less than twenty-four hours my response might border on the superficial.

However, speed was of the essence on the trip, for time is money. I had even travelled without Mike in order to eke out our dwindling budget. At least it was not my first encounter with caribou; in fact I felt quite familiar with them after three previous visits to their tundra home and, after many hours spent sitting in noisy jet planes, it was a relief to be out there alone, to see the space, smell the earth, hear the silence. The gently undulating land spread out on all sides, the hollows between the hills filled with lakes. Standing alone atop one of the hills, I realised that there was no human settlement between me and the North Pole. It is a wonderful feeling to experience so much space, and though aware of this thrill on previous occasions it is no less inspiring each time you realise there are still such places on this crowded planet.

Whilst walking the three kilometres to the caribou I had seen by the lake shore, I slowly became aware of my isolation and vulnerability. Grizzly bears roam the Barrens and they are notoriously unpredictable, even dangerous, and I wished I had a Magnum .44 strapped to my waist. Alert to the potential danger, I reached the brow of a hill when I was suddenly confronted by an animal. My heart leapt and the surprise immobilised us both for a moment, but it was a red fox, not a grizzly, and it turned tail and ran.

On that first day I saw several red foxes hurrying busily around. Being some 400 kilometres from the northern coast of Canada, I was too far south to encounter the smaller arctic fox, but the red fox looked magnificent with its thick russet coat and bushy tail streaming out behind as it ran.

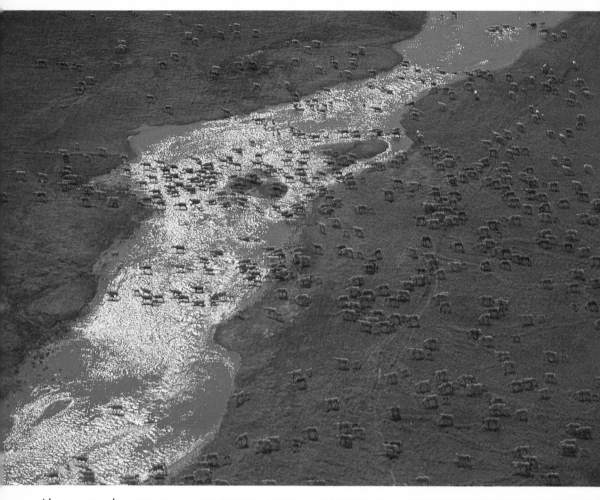

*Above: massed
caribou herds
move towards
the trees*

*Right: arctic fox
and arctic hare*

196

Walking on towards the lake shore, I approached the caribou slowly but they merely looked up and then continued their busy grazing. They were eating grass and lichen, along with the berries that had now ripened on the tundra plants. The berries comprise the Barren-Ground harvest that is so vital to all the Arctic's animals and birds. For those species that migrate, like snow buntings and horned larks, they provide protein-rich fuel for the journey south, and for the creatures that have to survive the rigours of a nine-month Arctic winter, they supply much of the food that will enable fat reserves to build up. I came across ptarmigan whose white breasts were stained pink by the juice from the red 'bear berry', and the caribou were positively rotund due to the glut.

The caribou looked magnificent in their fresh autumn coat, glistening with health, their backs dark brown, bellies nearly black, the bulls sporting a great white mane that hung down from their swollen, muscular necks. Some carried huge racks of antlers, red with blood as they shed their 'velvet' – the fluffy skin that protects the antlers during their season of growth. The velvet evidently irritated them for they thrashed the antlers on low bushes in order to rub it off. They looked so different from the thin, scrawny animals that we had seen filing wearily out of the trees in the spring. And so they should, for if they are not in good condition in the autumn, they will never survive the winter, let alone the rut. Some of the younger bulls were already testing out their new antlers on each other and establishing superiority in the herds, but the prime bulls were conserving their energy for the really serious fights that take place in mid-October.

Arctic hares were fairly numerous and widespread. They too fed busily on the berries and grasses, one particularly enterprising individual systematically stripping the seed heads off the grass as if it were an enthusiastic budgie. It must have learnt that seeds and berries would provide more nutrients than mere grass.

The hares had remained white all summer, and stood out starkly, but another resident mammal, the ground squirrel, was more appropriately coloured in rustic browns. They would have no need to turn white to remain camouflaged through the winter for, surprisingly, they are the one true hibernator of the Arctic. Having fattened up on lush summer vegetation and autumn berries, they sat in the sun by their holes, or stood upright on their hind legs, keeping a wary eye on the foxes, or on the rough-legged buzzards that drifted overhead on their southward migration. Winter was coming and once the snows arrived the ground squirrels would curl up in their nests and sleep until the thaw next June. The nest had already been prepared, dug into sandy ground during the summer, when the permafrost is at its greatest distance from the surface and before night frosts make the ground too hard. The nest chamber is insulated with dried grasses, gathered from the surrounding tundra.

Ground squirrels are the most sought-after inhabitants of the tundra, and the list of creatures that include them as a major part of their diet makes their existence somewhat precarious. They are not just foxes and buzzards but golden eagles, wolves, snowy owls, and most of all the grizzly bear. Although grizzlies have a very catholic diet which includes many berries, they spend hours digging up ground squirrel burrows in the hope of surprising the occupants. It was an activity I hoped to film, but the one bear I came across after a few days just ran off and did not stop for two kilometres; it was only a little one of 130–180 kilos, but big enough I thought!

After a promising start to the trip the weather turned really nasty, with low cloud, strong wind and sleet whipping across the open tundra. I stayed under cover and took advantage of the break to talk to the mine managers, Bob Gilroy and Gerry McCrank. They had made me very welcome and I had naturally become interested in the operation under whose roof I was shelter-ing, not least because of the controversy over the potential effects of a mine on the environment.

The Lupin Mine is Canada's second largest gold mine and is one of the highest-grade gold operations in North America. Situated as it is some 200 kilometres north of the tree-line in one of the world's most forbidding envir-onments, there are several problems that do not occur elsewhere. The build-ings have to withstand intense cold and high winds, the fuel bills to heat them are astronomic, and for nearly ten months of the year aircraft provide the only link between the mine and the outside world.

During the other two months, when the lake ice freezes to a thickness of a metre, construction crews set out from either end of the route to clear snow from the frozen land and lakes for the company's 600-kilometre winter ice-road. The road runs roughly south-west to Yellowknife and each year it takes six weeks to construct. Even then, travelling the road can sometimes be dangerous and drivers move in convoys and are prepared to abandon their trucks at the first sign of the lake ice cracking under the weight of the loads. For ten weeks in the depths of winter these trucks haul in twelve months' supply of fuel and bulk materials, the round trip taking three days. All other goods, including mining equipment and the buildings themselves, are flown in by Hercules transport plane.

Despite the isolation, the mine is in very good economic health and employs over 350 people. They mine the gold from underground shafts, the precious metal appearing as infinitesimal flecks in pockets of innocuous-looking grey rock. The rock is crushed into a fine powder, the gold dust separated by chemicals, then formed into those glistening bars so beloved by man the world over – the removal of 'souvenirs' is not encouraged!

Environmental considerations are becoming a more significant aspect of their budget, not least because of the removal of waste products, particularly the chemicals, which include arsenic. Ensuring this does not find its way into any of the water catchment of the Barrens has proved a major expense for the mines. The toxic water is firstly purified by chemicals and then a long pipeline takes it to a large hollow in the tundra, out of which no rivers flow. There it is allowed to settle behind impervious dams, and these 'tailing ponds' are the final process in preventing environmental pollution.

And the mine itself? Well, although the three-storey, bright-red buildings appear incongruous in the Arctic and the power plants and generators are noisy, if you step a few kilometres away the peace is restored. And you don't need to walk that far to see animals and birds. Hares were sheltering amongst the pipes, numerous migrant birds pecked for food amongst the buildings and were preyed on by three peregrine falcons. Several ground squirrels had decided to hibernate under the hot-water pipes, and caribou fed unconcerned in the shadow of the building and fuel tanks.

A major concern of conservationists is the effect of mines and pipelines on the migration routes of caribou and, though such activity and disturbance would be critical in the calving grounds, the caribou I watched in this area were totally unaffected. It is claimed they will not cross roads or pipelines, but I filmed them doing both, even jumping the pipes with not a moment's hesitation. It was a heartening sight. However, several scientists pointed out to us that, while most development is fine in many areas, the critical sites on which wildlife depends, such as nesting colonies and calving grounds, must be protected. Arctic wildlife is resilient – it has to be – but developers cannot afford to be complacent and the ones I met are not.

On 13 and 14 September a large number of caribou migrated south, just to the west of the mine. I saw more than a thousand early one morning and suspected they might be the last big herd. Several more rough-legged buzzards drifted south, arctic skuas likewise, and two families of whistling swans lingered only briefly on a nearby lake, perhaps the last migrants to flee the north.

The sun had now lost its warmth and had been sliding below the horizon for several nights, the first hours of darkness since early May. The nights had been cold, the frost rimming the ground, and birches, willows and plants had turned the most glorious colours: crimsons, ochres, yellows, vermilion, gold and russet browns. Amongst this celebration of death and decay, the ponds started to freeze, and each night's increment of frost was marked by lines in the ice, reminding me of the growth rings of a tree.

On 16 September the sky grew increasingly leaden and snow started to fall steadily. The reds were turned white and the last of the caribou filed past with heads bowed, their backs turning ever whiter. They seemed aware that there is an inevitability about the coming of winter and I felt sad as I watched them depart over the far horizon. The Arctic summer was over, seeds set, the harvest gathered in, and the colourful tundra would soon become blanketed by the snows of a long, hard winter.

Mission accomplished, I too headed south, flying over the caribous' heads in a small Cessna. As we had floats for lake landings and both the pilot and I are keen fishermen, we broke the journey back to Yellowknife to hunt a few trout. Picking a likely-looking spot, we splashed down, and cast our lines out, using the plane's floats as a fishing platform. We were immediately catching fish, dozens of them, mostly lake trout weighing about one kilo but with a few equally large grayling. They are attractive fish, their silvery flanks flushed with pink and their large dorsal fin extended like a sail – they are known affectionately as the 'ladies of the stream'. The fishing seemed fantastic, the atmosphere

*Above and right:
caribou in a
land of lakes*

200

Above: the colour of autumn

Left: large bull caribou and more autumn beauty

201

peaceful, musty with the attractive smell of autumn leaves and fungus. The day was made complete when a bald eagle circled overhead, then drifted away over the golden trees. Lost in this dream world, I was suddenly jerked into consciousness when the rod was nearly wrenched out of my hand, straining alarmingly. A long, hard battle was fought before the trout tired and, excited at its size, I lifted it carefully aboard. It weighed five kilos and must have been at least thirty-two years old. Growth is slow in those icy lakes and the trout are only able to build their condition sufficiently to breed once every two to three years. I could not kill a veteran of that size, survivor of so many Arctic winters. So we took a couple of smaller ones for our supper and watched the leviathan swim slowly away into the depths of the cold, clear lake. There would be comfort to know that he still swam there when I returned to film the caribou rut in a month's time.

I travelled home to England the next day, and within a week I was back in North Africa. The sun shone down as I filmed flamingos and wildfowl on Lake Ichkeul in Tunisia. The heat was a contrast to the wintry Arctic and, when I returned to Canada on 14 October, I received an even bigger shock to the system. On disembarking from my flight to Yellowknife, I was greeted by a horizontal blizzard. This was extremely unwelcome, for we planned to camp with the caribou as they migrated into the trees, and film the rut that takes place during their journey.

We were to be in a remote area of the Barrens, about 200 kilometres north-east of Yellowknife, so I had booked a small helicopter and arranged for all our fuel, tents and food to be flown ahead and dumped at a prearranged spot. Space in the helicopter would be very limited, so just myself and the pilot would fly the mission.

'No one knows the ways of the wind or the caribou' is an old and appropriate proverb, for the fuel dump was strategically placed to ensure the caribou were nowhere near the area we chose! The choice was not entirely random, however, for in their journey from the calving grounds back to the trees, the caribou travel in a roughly south-westerly direction, and in so doing come across the vast expanse of Contwoyto and MacKay Lakes. These act as a partial barrier and tend to drive the bulk of the herd either to east or west. From there the caribou continue south-west for 200 kilometres, making for the area of Jordan Lake, where they spend the winter. Caribou can wander anywhere they like, and do, so the scenario I have drawn is a gross over-simplification, but it is a useful theory because it narrows down the search – a search which is almost impossible because the area is so vast and the caribou so elusive.

In the past many film-makers and biologists have tried to find them and failed. Even the Inuit, who rely on the caribou for food and clothing, have also failed to locate them and whole families have died as a consequence. Finding caribou was not quite a matter of life or death for us, but time was not on our side either, for the peak of the rut takes place over just five days.

Mike and I had been beaten the previous year when a blizzard raged for five days, grounding our helicopter. When we had finally become airborne, the caribou were in the area we had calculated, but the peak of the rut was over, with most of the leading stags sitting around in a state of apparent exhaustion. It was a big disappointment and our first major failure; I hoped to avoid a repeat. However, the blizzard that had greeted me on the 14th continued, and I began to fear the worst. Fortunately, on the morning of 16 October we managed to take off in a small Cessna and start a new search for the caribou.

The weather was windy but clear as we flew north-east of Yellowknife. The ground was tree-covered, but the hollows became ever more thinly scattered with the hardy spruce, bent and gnarled by the wind. We were at their northern limit of growth and once we had crossed this tree-line they petered out altogether and we were left with a monotonous white infinity. Flurries of snow blew across the flattened tundra, all but obliterating the deep-cut tracks of generations of migrating caribou, but no animal looked up to watch our passing, no bird flew before our own stiff and lifeless wings. Nothing stirred except the ruffled surface of the lakes, tormented by the fierce breeze. It was well below freezing and the smaller lakes were already frozen.

Only the previous year Mike and I had travelled this same route and found the caribou in their hundreds and thousands. But now, as we reached our fuel and food dump at Lac Tête d'Ours, 'the lake of the head of the bear', we knew in our hearts that we would not find them there in 1984. That would be too easy! Nevertheless, we had to continue the search and followed their ancient track north.

Flying over that white wilderness, with time to think, your imagination runs riot. There are so many lakes – albeit frozen now – seemingly insignificant, but not to someone, sometime. There are those named after explorers, travellers and trappers, not only MacKay but McCrea, McVicar, and McTavish. Then there are those associated with animals – Buffalo Lake, Great Bear, Nanook, Musk Ox, Whitewolf, Lynx, Wolverine, and even the lowly mosquito has a lake named after it. There are also amusing anatomical ones like Long Legs Lake, Crooked Foot, Little Forehead, Baldhead, Nose, and Fingers Lake. Then there are those that must tell a story, like Cache Lake, Hunger Lake, Desperation Lake, Starvation Lake and Lac du Mort! All that activity at some time in history, but on the day of our search nothing stirred, the land had only a past, no present – the snow was lifeless.

If there were no caribou to the east, they must be way to the west. So we headed that way, searching around Lac de Gras en route, and finding fresh caribou tracks to the west of the lake. Then at last some caribou. There were just a few, the back markers perhaps, so we followed the fresh tracks south but eventually they petered out. We had only seen some thirty animals and there should have been thousands. We had been flying for three and a half hours and only had a range of four and a half. Yellowknife was nearly an hour away – Desperation Lake was appropriate! We decided to head home in a wide westerly curve, past Jolly Lake, then towards Winter Lake. We had reached the area of Snare River when more fresh tracks became evident, then a scattering of caribou, then more caribou. We became ever more excited and just as we reached the limit of our fuel before having to turn back, we found the 'mother lode': hundreds and hundreds of caribou trekking slowly south, scattered across the tundra in loose lines about a mile across and several miles long. We even saw a wolf with them which convinced us we had found the main herd.

There was no time for a thorough count, we had to fly directly home, but the relief of finding them was enormous and the thrill of anticipation intense. There were plans to make, of course, for the fuel and camping gear were over 100 kilometres to the east. But only 50 kilometres from the caribou is another gold mine called Salmita, and we would ask if we could use that as a base. They had made Mike and me very welcome when we stayed there to film the rut the previous year, and when we phoned them on our return to Yellowknife they again welcomed us. So now we knew where the caribou were, we had a base and a helicopter and were raring to go, and just like the previous year the weather grounded us again – another blizzard. We prayed for a break and on 18 October we got it, so by 9.30 a.m. the helicopter was airborne, piloted by Dave McCuaig. On board we had our filming equipment, also food, cooking equipment and survival gear, just in case we became grounded by the weather. It is notoriously unreliable in the Barrens during the onset of winter.

We found the caribou again after flying for two hours. They had travelled some 30 kilometres south towards the trees, so at a rate of migration of 14 kilometres a day we hoped it would not be difficult for us to find them each day. We circled high above them to avoid disturbance, flew beyond the front of the herd, calculated where they might head, and landed behind a hill, on the side of which was an isolated clump of spruce. This would be our hide.

*Bull caribou
fight violently
during the rut*

*Above: the
Bathurst Herd
reaches the trees*

*Left: filming
at the tree-line*

We had not been concealed long before the first few caribou appeared on the skyline and headed directly towards us. They were moving purposefully but unhurriedly, for they stopped frequently, thrusting their noses through the soft snow to feed on lichens. The northerly wind carried our scent away from them, so we remained undetected. Ever more caribou appeared, not just in front of us, but to either side as far as we could see from the edge of our hill. The leading animals walked on past us and continued south, so we were now in the heart of the migrating herd. The tundra seemed to flow with them, a river of life three kilometres wide. Surrounded by thousands of animals, you would expect a lot of sound, but caribou travel noiselessly, the uncanny silence broken only by the clicking of their kneecaps. This might appear to be a joke, but those who have been lucky enough to travel with the caribou and experience this wonderful spectacle will know that it is true.

We were naturally anxious to discover whether the rut had started, or whether we were too late, for though the five-day event is said to start on about 22 October, I had had a hunch that I ought to be around earlier than that. As the animals filed past there was no apparent sign that anything was going to happen – maybe it was already over. We stood dreading the worst, when I began to notice signs of subtle behaviour; a large bull persistently following a cow and, when she stopped to feed, standing close by, with legs tucked in below him. He would stare at the ground intently, as if concentrating very hard, then would urinate and tread that into the snow. The moment the cow moved off so would the bull, and occasionally he would raise his head in the air with mouth slightly open, nostrils flared, eyes closed in bliss as he caught the scent of a cow in heat.

No sooner had we convinced ourselves that we had not missed the biggest event of the year on the Canadian tundra than two bulls burst into the small valley in hot pursuit of a cow. When alongside they suddenly wheeled on each other and locked antlers with an explosive rattle, breaking the silence in staccato fashion and causing the snow to fly. They pushed and twisted briefly, then disengaged and continued to chase the cow, who headed south-west towards the evening sky. All three clattered across a freshly frozen lake just to our left and disappeared over a ridge, starting a procession of more sedate travellers who gingerly headed onto the treacherous lake. It had been calm when the water froze so the surface was very smooth and slippery. One calf skidded along on its behind in comical cartoon fashion, and a cow fell through the ice near the lake edge and struggled to extricate herself. But in time their numerous sharp hooves etched a safe path across the ice, and hundreds poured along the same route in straggling lines. The pace of migration was evidently increasing towards late afternoon and rutting activity had largely been adjourned. In the evening, calls of wolves echoed over the northern horizon and we waited with anticipation for them to appear. But the day's end reached us before them, the sun set, dusk closed in quickly and we flew east to Salmita in the twilight of an Arctic night.

Salmita Mine site seems to have little direct influence on the caribou migration, but the winter road into Yellowknife that they share with Lupin

Mine does on occasions prove a problem. It is not the mine's fault that their essential link with the outside world also provides easy access to the wilderness for those who wouldn't otherwise take the trouble to go. In January and February 1984, the caribou herds chose to migrate close to the ice-road, and every man and his dog jumped into their pick-ups, drove along the winter road and massacred as many animals as they could carry. The government controls hunting on a strict quota system but this was mayhem. The law was clearly being broken, but the authorities had insufficient resources to enforce the quotas. Once the hunters' freezers were full, they were going out and killing caribou just for the sake of a few tasty morsels like the tongues. The road edge was littered with heaps of frozen carcasses, a sad memorial to the dangers of uncontrolled access to the Arctic.

Such a tragedy would never have happened in the days when the Inuit carried out subsistence hunting, for they could not afford to waste their animals. Even today, their hunting is nearly always based on need, not greed, and flying over the Barrens, we saw the tracks of their skidoos circling red patches in the snow. Such killing might seem distasteful to urban man although, if you live on the land, taking available and appropriate harvest makes sense, but massacres that destroy populations – be they of caribou, whales or herring – are a crime against humanity, whoever is responsible.

19 October dawned, another 'diamond day' as my pilot Dave McCuaig called it, and we were heading west from the mine even before daybreak. Timing our journey the previous night we knew that it would take us thirty-five minutes' flying time to reach the caribou, and by then it would be light enough to see them.

We soon spotted their dark backs against the snow and dropped down just ahead of them onto a hilltop amongst a few trees. As soon as the noisy rotor blades had stopped we became aware of wolves calling, and scanning with binoculars, I discovered them on a rocky hilltop about a kilometre away. There were three or four of them, pure white and quite magnificent as they sat on the skyline, throwing their heads back as they howled that haunting cry.

Grabbing the camera, I set off through the dense spruce forest, hoping I could stalk close enough to film them. I decided to leave the rifle behind as the extra encumbrance would make the approach even more difficult. The rifle was not to protect me from the wolves, but from grizzly bears. We had seen fresh tracks and bears were likely to be active on such a fine morning. The further I walked from the helicopter the more exposed to danger I felt; it was not just the exertion of the stalk which was causing me to sweat! Much to my surprise, the wolves allowed me quite close and I filmed and recorded them calling before they filtered away into the frost-rimmed trees; white on white, they disappeared like ghosts. This exciting experience was to make the opening of our film about the tundra, for the scene was made into a fairy-tale land by the bushes covered with hoar-frost and ice crystals sparkling in the chill air at sunrise.

By the time I had returned to the helicopter the caribou had filled the meadow below the hill and the rut was evidently now in full swing. The scene was like a rodeo, with bulls charging around at a gallop and snow flying in all directions as they chased the cows as fast as they could run. Bull caribou do not defend harems like most deer, but accept that any cow in heat is fair game, and compete for her favours. Up to six bulls were chasing after one particular cow and it struck me that if she would just stand still she might save everybody a lot of trouble. She herself grunted and panted with the exertion, let alone the bulls, who were gasping for breath and fighting in real earnest.

Their enormous antlers clashed frequently that morning, the contests being serious battles of strength in which the competitors shoved and twisted for minutes at a time, trying either to knock the other off its feet, to gouge it with its antlers, or preferably to push it off the planet. Muscles strained, whites of eyes rolled and blood flowed. Two days of these battles saw several animals limping badly, another had a gash in its side and one had a nasty throat wound which left a trail of blood in the snow. The injured ones would not make it through the winter, for the wolves follow the herds throughout the year and very quickly thin out the weak and injured. Ravens flew over the herds too, making a living on pickings from wolf kills, and one big bull that had fought its last fight was already being attacked hungrily by twelve black angels of death.

Not just the injured die, for the bulls spend fourteen weeks storing fat reserves and waste it away in just one week. The short, violent, exhausting rut means they enter the harsh winter in poor condition. But at least the needs of the species have been served and the cows mated by the most powerful and aggressive bulls. The caribou looked very tired that last evening as they drifted south into the gathering darkness of the trees; they had reached the winter quarters and their year was now complete. We had filmed the final sequence for the tundra film and we too trudged away through the snow. Wolves howled in the twilight – they would feed well that night.

Wolves follow caribou back into the trees

FAREWELL TO THE GREAT WHITE BEAR

In early winter, as the caribou head south-west into the trees, the polar bears are doing just the opposite, moving purposelessly northwards away from the trees around Hudson Bay and out on to the newly formed sea ice. So, on 21 October 1984, I left the Barren Grounds to the caribou, flew back to Yellowknife, repacked the filming gear, and on the 23rd was heading for Churchill, the famous town on the western shores of Hudson Bay that boasts to be the 'polar bear capital of the world'.

I had never really wanted to visit this great centre for tourism because it has never struck me as being truly 'Arctic' in the wilderness sense – it is too accessible. Churchill can be reached by road, rail, sea and air, and at one time or another it seemed that every cameraman in the world had visited it to photograph polar bears. However, no sooner had I flown in to the busy airport than I was flying back out again, heading 50 kilometres east to Cape Churchill, a prominent headland that juts out into Hudson Bay.

The shallow waters of Hudson Bay are a good place for ringed seals which naturally means it is also a good place for polar bears, but in the summer, when the sea ice melts, the bears have to come ashore. They wander the coast and tundra just inland, subsisting on a meagre diet of vegetation and berries. But they hardly eat anything for several months and use some of their fat reserves to stay alive, so by late October they are hungry, and keen to get their teeth into a nice fat seal. However, they must wait for the sea to freeze, and Cape Churchill is one of the first places where this happens. A combination of the headland and tides concentrates the newly formed ice floes at the Cape, and the bears migrate north and congregate here to await the coming of winter.

It seemed winter had already arrived as I flew east in a little Cessna, for the ponds and sea edge were already frozen, the ground was powdered with snow and the stormy sky threatened even more. We landed at the Cape with some

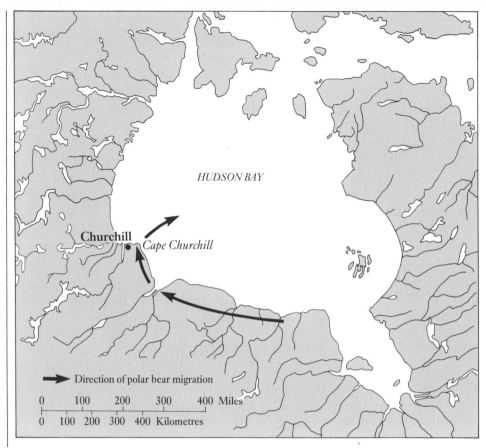

HUDSON BAY

Churchill

Cape Churchill

➤ Direction of polar bear migration

| 0 | 100 | 200 | 300 | 400 Miles |
| 0 | 100 | 200 | 300 | 400 Kilometres |

difficulty, for the wind had risen to near gale force and was across our line of approach. What was more, it was snowing heavily and the landing strip was a loose gravel ridge, but we bumped down without mishap and threw off my inevitable mountain of gear. I had not had time to change from my city clothes after my flight from Yellowknife, and the bitter cold wind bit deep. However, the warmth of greeting from my future companions overcame any sense of chilly isolation and we soon had the gear stowed and the coffee pot percolating.

I had been met by Andy Derocher and Steve Miller. Andy is a research student with Dr Ian Stirling, and Steve an ace helicopter pilot who had flown thousands of hours all over the Arctic whilst marking polar bears. He had taken leave from flying in order to spend some time watching bears instead of chasing them. So Andy and Steve were both part of Ian's 'flying circus', as it is affectionately known in the Arctic, and it was thanks to Ian that I had been allowed to join the team.

The accommodation comprised·a single room, three metres square, in which some of the space was already taken up by a cooking bench, several shelves, and a most welcome oil stove. Sleeping would be done on the floor, sardine fashion. Outside was a balcony on which stood a bucket as a chemical toilet – a draughty prospect – and all of this was perched on a tower, 14 metres above the ground. Further down the rickety-looking structure was a large platform on which was stacked all my filming gear, the food, and a generator for battery charging. Everything had to be stowed out of reach of the bears, and whilst they were close by, we could not step off our island home.

Andy and Steve had seen nine bears that morning, the first day when appreciable numbers were around, so it seemed my arrival was fortuitously timed. We could not watch the bears that evening, for the weather had deteriorated to such an extent that we could barely see the ground. Instead, we whiled away the evening talking about the Arctic in general and bears in particular. Andy and Steve were at Cape Churchill on behalf of the North-west Territories' government, carrying out research into so-called 'problem bears'. With the increase of industrial exploration and other forms of human activity in areas of bear habitat, there has been an increase in interaction between bears and humans. Such encounters can jeopardise human safety, cause loss of property and, in instances where problem bears are killed, place additional stress on their populations. For example, the number of 'nuisance' polar bear kills in the Northwest Territories has been steadily increasing since 1977, when ten bears were killed, to 1982 when forty-two were killed – and these are the ones we know about. These losses to the population are in addition to the quota of bears that each settlement is licensed to take each year.

In 1981, a programme was initiated by industry and government to develop safe and practical techniques to detect and deter bears and thus reduce the number of nuisance kills and increase human safety. Andy was continuing the research and, as he explained, 'What we are looking for is a way in which polar bears and man can co-exist in the Arctic, so we need a deterrent to keep polar bears away from inhabited areas without permanent damage to the animal. We are dealing with an extremely curious animal, and they will quite often approach inhabited areas. They are attracted by the smells of cooking and garbage and, though that does not necessarily constitute a threat, most people just do not want a potentially very dangerous animal nosing around. An effective deterrent would punish a bear for venturing near to human activity and, once the bear has learned that it gets punished for being an intruder, it will hopefully no longer venture into such areas.

'We are carrying out a series of trials using a 12-gauge shotgun and a plastic projectile that we can shoot at the bear. There is no permanent damage to the animal; it certainly does not penetrate the thick fur, but it inflicts enough of a shock and a bit of a punch that will move the animal out of the area. The projectiles are effective in the range of roughly 20–30 metres, but anything greater than that distance, given high winds and the light nature of the projectile, and the accuracy is insufficient. We attract the bears for tests by baiting anchored fuel drums with seal oil, and about 25 metres away we have a safety cage into which we can escape if a bear approaches too closely.

'Throughout the summer, we have been marking bears in this area with large black letters so we can check if individuals return after they have been deterred. Some do, but we have a slightly false situation because, regardless of bait, the bears want to be here anyway, waiting to go out on the ice. However, we obviously have the makings of a good deterrent.'

It struck me that there was one snag with the deterrent, and that was 'range'. For most people a polar bear at 25 metres would appear a dangerous and frightening spectacle. It certainly was for me at first, but like everyone else who takes an interest in the Arctic I had been indoctrinated by all the stories of people being killed and eaten by bears, about bears terrorising towns, stalking scientists, chasing explorers, tearing down camps and cabins, in fact causing mayhem throughout the north. I suspect some of the polar bear's reputation for being dangerous has been created purely to enhance the 'macho' image of some of those who have worked in the Arctic, and there are certainly some appalling recent examples in the media of the bear's false image as a 'man-eater' being perpetrated for personal and monetary gain – 'Gee, they are really trying to get ya' echoes loudly in the memory.

This somewhat false reputation has done nothing for the polar bear, and no doubt it has led to bears being shot even when they posed no threat at all. Certainly they can be dangerous if allowed to approach too closely, for even a playful swat with their massive paws can knock you senseless. But over three years, a growing familiarity with the sensation of being close to bears has made me aware that they are not trying to eat you at every opportunity but are merely inquisitive. There is no doubt, however, that a polar bear at 25 metres is impressive, even a young one, not so much because of their size, but their 'presence', their loose-limbed grace, their relaxed confidence. Words I have used in my diary to describe them are docile, dignified and even distinguished, and they are one of those animals that always demand attention, even command it. They have 'charisma' and it is not by chance that they have been called 'Lords of the Arctic', 'His Majesty', and 'King of the North'. Watching them in their own environment of snow and ice has been one of the greatest privileges of my life.

During the night the storm abated and 25 October dawned clear and bright. As I wrote in my diary, 'It has been a wonderful day surrounded by bears – took some useful film but nothing knock-out.' This extract highlights the major snag of working at Cape Churchill: the number of bears that have been marked with black lettering for research purposes. We naturally wanted to avoid filming these 'tainted' bears, and opportunities on that first day were limited. However, the bears were numerous and, although at dawn we could see only two, as the day progressed they seemed to appear mysteriously out of every snow bank and bush.

Our tower-top home was perched amongst a series of gravel beach ridges, the hollows between comprising freshwater lakes and ponds and dense pockets of sedge and willow scrub. We were at the edge of the tree-line, so the willow was large enough to hide any number of bears and certainly supported flocks of ptarmigan numbering thirty to forty. They flew from willow to willow like snowflakes across the already white, powdered ground. To the east lay the sea, an unfrozen steely grey, the shoreline dotted with ice floes. To the west, the large brackish lake was already frozen, and a bear walked

*The tower at
Cape Churchill*

*Male bears in
playful mood*

213

cautiously on its new surface, moving forward tentatively for fear of falling through.

Bears arrived at the Cape all day, some out of the bushes where they must have slept the night, others from several kilometres down the coast, heading north to join the throng. Andy tells me a gathering of bears is called a 'sloth', a somewhat disparaging description for such an exciting event, for one of the consequences of this rare gathering is the spectacle of bears playing in the snow. Out on the ice, bears usually avoid each other, the only exception I heard of being a gathering of fifty-two around a whale carcass in Svalbard. But at Cape Churchill, bears of equal size seem to seek each other out and the only sensible explanation for this is that they enjoy a good romp.

On the first day we saw two magnificent males of about six years old walk towards each other on a snow bank. After circling for several minutes and sniffing each other's faces, to the accompaniment of occasional low growls and much very quiet muttering – they were certainly communicating by both sight and sound – one suddenly lunged forward, grabbed the other by the foreleg and wrestled it into the snow. There followed a wonderful ten minutes of entertainment as each in turn tried to gain the ascendancy, their ultimate purpose seemingly to pin the other to the ground. There was much biting of neck and ears, apart from front and back legs, and many comical occasions when legs waved in the air. Most impressive of all were the occasions when one would escape from a hold, then both would rear up on their hind legs and, standing some two metres high, would box each other around the ears, powdery snow flying from their coats and paws in great clouds. Although all this sounds vicious and violent, it always appeared to be totally good-natured, and once they had exhausted each other they would often bed down together in a snowdrift and sleep for several hours. Thus the bears would while away the days in play and indolent slumber, interspersed with pacing over to the coast to see if the ice had formed.

Each day new bears were recruited into the 'playgroup' from the south and, with several bears roaming around the tower, we sometimes had a problem climbing down on to the ground to film. One young bear chose to sleep right below the ladder, so as there seemed to be little else to throw at it, I tried snowballs. I was disappointed when it did not throw any back!

One delightful incident which highlighted the inquisitiveness of polar bears involved the rope which hung down from the top of the tower to lower equipment. One morning this was blowing about in a gale about two metres from the ground. A young bear walked up, stood on its hind legs and, just like a playful kitten, was trying to catch the end of the rope. At mealtimes our cabin became the focus of attention, and for one young bear the smell of bacon and eggs was almost too much. He paced up and down below the window, sniffing the air in hunger, then, noticing a stack of fuel drums, climbed up on top of them and stood on his hind legs like a circus act.

One really impressive male was not quite so comical. We knew him as 'Foxtrot Charlie', for on 11 August he had been caught by Andy and Steve some 140 kilometres to the south and marked with the letters FC. He was about sixteen years old, massively built, with a huge grizzled head, scarred from numerous mating battles, and a nasty old wound right across one eye – we wondered if he could still see out of it, for his eyeball was bloodshot.

As we stood in the safety cage one day, this mean-looking, but merely inquisitive male walked up to us, and though we were standing upright and he was on all fours, he still looked us straight in the eye. An eyeball to eyeball confrontation with a bear of that size scarcely a metre away, even with bars between you, is very impressive; especially when he stood up at well over two metres and started pounding on the bars. He completely dwarfed us, but we had no fear, for there was no malevolence in his bloodshot gaze, only inquisitive interest and a keenness to reach the whale oil we had stored in a drum. It was a wonderful experience to be so close to such a powerful animal, and comical to have the tables turned, for instead of the usual zoo experience where we stare at a caged wild animal, we were caged up ourselves, and being looked at with great interest.

That night, as we cooked supper up in the tower, 'Foxtrot Charlie' caught the scent and, knowing where the goodies were, tried to shake them out of the cabin! He pounded on the tower as we cooked, then woke us again at night, the substantial structure, 14 metres high, rocking under the power of his blows, and the mugs swinging on their hooks in the ceiling. I was glad he had not visited us in our tent on Svalbard!

We got to know several other bears by name. One was 'Head Mount', recognisable from the marks on his fur where a transmitter was once attached for scientific tracking purposes. Then there were two young bears, 'Racoon' and 'Three Eyes', recognisable from black marks on their white fur. Racoon was quite a character, for he hung around the tower and bait site for several days and we had long since stopped trying to deter him with projectiles. It is often these small, sub-adult bears that become 'problem bears' – the juvenile delinquents of the Arctic – for they know no fear, and Racoon would often see off male bears twice his size if he wanted a feed from the bait.

On 29 October we had a visit from a planeful of tourists from Churchill. They did not land, but circled the Cape so the occupants could watch the bears. They had to go to this expense to see bears as the 'polar bear capital of the world' had no polar bears – they had all been locked up 'in jail'! There was considerable anger in Churchill amongst tourists, for they had spent thousands of dollars travelling there and had to make a long bumpy ride out of town in a tundra buggy to see one. The hoteliers were worried about their livelihood, for tourism brings two or three million dollars into Churchill every year, most of those earnings being directly attributable to bears. However, the town council had decided they no longer wanted large carnivores wandering the streets of Churchill. So the bears had been tranquillised and put in the holding pens called D20; they would be released from 'jail' on to the ice when it had formed.

The only bear near town in 1984 became affectionately known as 'CV' – the name coined from the letters on her side, and the affection due to the enjoyment the four-year-old had given to so many people. Then, on 4

November, even that bear had gone, shot 'in self-defence' by four young lads out ptarmigan shooting. The hoteliers were even more angry, and sceptical, for they too wondered why the lads were on the shore if they were really out ptarmigan shooting. If Dr Ian Stirling can spend twenty years working with bears in the Arctic without ever having to shoot one, it seems likely that at least a proportion of 'defence kills' are totally unnecessary.

Several locals I spoke to who had lived in Churchill for some time were rather scathing about the concept of 'problem bears', reckoning it was the humans who were the problem. 'The bears had migrated through this area long before a town was here,' they said, 'and they are no problem as long as you are sensible.' One great idea was to start a pig farm in the area – it no longer exists, however, as the bears decided it was great having bacon for breakfast!

The Churchill rubbish dump naturally attracts hungry bears, but even these had been locked up in 1984. It struck me as hardly fair to spread out all those tempting morsels in the path of migrating bears, then lock them up for doing what comes naturally. Better still to have fenced the dump in the first place, for old habits die hard and one famous twenty-year-old bear called Linda has been visiting the dump since 1976. Every other year she brings her new cubs, and they learn the habit too. The routine has also highlighted the difference between Hudson Bay bears and others throughout the Arctic, for Linda and other bears are able to breed every two years, whereas elsewhere throughout the Arctic the cubs are dependent on their parents for two and a half years. This means the adults are unable to breed again until the third year.

The reasons why Hudson Bay bears are different is complex, and still the subject of several research projects. But one theory is that the better feeding available near the tree-line – when the bears are ashore in the summer – enables the females to remain in good condition for breeding. Further north the land is largely a barren desert but around Hudson Bay there is lush vegetation in many places, and lots of nutritious berries.

At the Cape we saw one five-year-old male lie down and eat grass. He scratched up a tussock with his paw, chewed for some time and did not seem to swallow, so when he had moved off a little way I went to check, and found the masticated remains lying frozen in the snow. We also found bear droppings composed of grass, so sometimes they must swallow their apparently unappetising meal.

We got to know this grass-eating bear quite well, for he was with us for more than a week, and we could recognise him just by his pristine yellow-white coat and his magnificent condition. He was very playful, and we filmed him romping with several other big males. He also became quite tame, so much so that from the safety of the cage I was able to distract him by stroking his nose whilst Andy read the tag tucked discreetly inside his ear. The number was 9281 and he had been born in 1980 and caught at the Cape in 1982. Such tagging is invaluable for estimating population numbers and density, rates of survival and recruitment, for on this evidence is based the conservation of the polar bear throughout the Arctic. At four years old, '9281' was a youngster,

Bears will eat seaweed when very hungry

Waiting for the sea to freeze

217

the most elderly bear so far recorded being thirty-two years old. It weighed 803 kilos when caught in 1984 and would have stood nearly three metres high. Males tend to be larger than females and with so many big males around the Cape, females with cubs tend to stay away due to the harassment they might receive.

One exception at the Cape in 1984 was 'Q' and 'Q-bar', a mother and one-year-old cub that were often attracted to the bait and would 'gang up' and, running side by side, charge at large males. They made an impressive pair as they made the snow fly, and not one single male stood up to this onslaught — they just fled. I was glad not to be on the receiving end but it was 'Q' who gave me my only anxious moment in ten days surrounded by bears. I was on top of our safety cage doing some filming when 'Q-bar' the cub came up to investigate. That was no problem, but 'Q' became anxious and then started making aggressive signs, lowering her top lip and head and neck, accompanying this by a smacking of the lips and then sharp hisses. It was the preliminary to a charge and I felt somewhat exposed and wished I had been *in* the cage. But the cub moved away, 'Q' relaxed and the tension subsided.

By 29 October we had twenty-six bears in view at once, twelve of which were in the vicinity of our tower. They appeared to have a 'diurnal rhythm', being very active for two to three hours after sunrise, then taking a siesta for a couple of hours after lunch, before a final burst of activity in the evening. This would continue until we shut down at about 11 p.m., their ghostly white forms moving around in the torchlight. Judging by the numerous fresh tracks in the snow at dawn, they were often active during much of the night as well. This routine was followed when the weather was reasonably sunny and not too windy, but when a gale raged they would lie low.

One of the criticisms levelled at our previous Arctic film material was that it did not look harsh enough. Though we had filmed on numerous occasions in temperatures below −20°C and down to −46°C, the difference between that and −2°C does not show on film. What we needed was a good blizzard, so I was delighted when we experienced several at Cape Churchill. In fact the weather during much of my stay there could be described as dreadful, so we got some lovely film of the bears' reaction to these situations.

Once the wind was strong enough to lift the snow off the tundra and create a 'white-out', the bears would head for the bushes and, choosing the most substantial snowdrifts, start digging. They have huge, spade-like front paws, and with these they could shift a barrow load of snow at a time. They would soon have a hole large enough to accommodate them, and after pounding down the floor by jumping on it several times, would bed down, lay their chins on the snow, and go to sleep. The snow would then blow over them until they completely disappeared.

Being careful not to tread on a live lump of 'snow', we stalked up on '9281' who had just bedded down. We hoped to film him being covered with snow and managed to do so. He even lifted his head from under the snow right on cue, yawned, looked at us sleepily, then snuggled down and was once again covered by the blizzard.

He must have known what was coming, for that night blew up the worst storm I have ever experienced. During two years in the Arctic we had never really been hit by a bad blow, but the night of 29 October made up for it. Steve estimated the wind speed to be 60 mph – a hurricane – and what with the noise of the wind, the creaking and vibrating of the tower and the shaking of the hut, we had a horrendous night. I felt particularly vulnerable on top of a 14-metre tower, for having filmed various subjects from the tops of flimsy scaffolds I have a recurrent nightmare which wakes me up as the structure is falling. On this night the nightmare was real, for I was wide awake and sweating. I tried to sleep, but my mind raced with the implications of what might happen if the tower did get blown over. If the fall did not kill us then surely the cold or the dozen bears waiting below would.

I tried to put such foolish thoughts out of my mind, but as each severe gust shook the hut and equipment fell off the shelves, consciousness returned. Then at 2 a.m. there was a particularly strong gust and a loud bang from down below. Thinking one of the struts had snapped I was up in a second and shining a torch out of the window. Despite the weight of my equipment, and all our boxes of food and ropes and wires holding it down, the large wooden platform three sections below had blown apart. It was now jammed against the upright, and equipment and food scattered in the snow below. It would be too dangerous to try to do anything in the dark so we just hoped the bears would not wake and waited for the morning.

We survived the night, but the hurricane blew all next day, and it was hardly possible to stand up as we collected the film equipment and food from the snowdrifts. There was no sign of bears, but in the blizzard we stood back to back, one working, the other watching for bears, armed with a gun. Visibility was just five metres and a chance confrontation might be fatal. I felt sure my foolish thoughts about survival the night before had been mine alone, but on comparing notes we had all felt in danger. So, interspersed with warming up in the hut, we built a snow shelter and put survival rations and a gun in it. We even radioed a message to Churchill, explaining that if we did not make a radio schedule the next morning at 9 a.m. they were to send a rescue helicopter as soon as possible. In the event the storm finally blew itself out after just one more wild night and the only casualties were our frayed nerves.

As soon as it was light we could see that the wind had blown a large quantity of ice into the bay, and as each bear woke and poked its nose out of the snowdrifts, they too sensed the change and headed onto the ice floes to investigate. The ice was still too fragmentary for permanent residence, so the bears returned and played once more. '9281' came back to his usual snowdrift and plunged into it with gay abandon, as a child might run and jump into a swimming pool. He did the most amazing acrobatics, rolling ball-like somersaults, sliding on his belly with his behind in the air, propelled by his back legs, then scrubbing his back with a branch from a nearby bush. He was like a character from a Walt Disney cartoon, and every bit as funny.

He eventually settled down for a good sleep and seemed quite comfortable in the frosty darkness. Next morning, after a night of sharp frost and

219

blissful calm, the ice floes had frozen together, so on 1 November the bears started walking cautiously out into the bay. They had in prospect a meal of ringed seals, and the darkness of a polar winter.

I watched them depart on to the shimmering ice with regret, reflecting how Mike and I had changed our attitude to the great white bears. At first we faced them with fear and apprehension, now with confidence and affection. They are gentle giants, playful and inquisitive, not the aggressive killers that their reputation demands.

And has our attitude to the Arctic also changed? Well, now the films are finished they are something of a disappointment, for there is an inevitable compromise between one's imagination and reality. But the sense of fulfilment and privilege is intense, affection for the Arctic increased. We have shared many wonderful experiences, and most of these would have been impossible without the generous help of many good people. And despite the cold and hardship, the long separations from family and friends, the loneliness and risks, we remember it all with a longing to return and do it all again. That appears to be the obsession from which no Arctic traveller ever escapes, and our profound hope is that we have shared our privilege in both book and films, and maybe done a little to show people the wonders of the Arctic. Maybe we've even convinced a few that it is worth preserving, unspoiled, unfenced, undisturbed.

Apart from the animals and birds, the flowers and insects, the spectacular landscapes, the drifting ice, the dazzling light, the cold and dark, the Arctic can provide an abundance of that priceless – but to some worthless – commodity called wilderness. It is a place where man can be himself again, alone, primitive perhaps, but above all an individual. Humans need such experiences; they also need unspoilt spaces like the Arctic. It would be nice to think that we could leave this largest wilderness on earth intact. But the fact that it still exists, circling the northern globe in white infinity – that is inspiring, and that is what inspired the poet Robert Service, and ourselves:

> Have you ever heard of the Land of Beyond?
> That dreams at the gates of the day?
> Alluring it lies at the skirts of the skies,
> and ever so far away.

LIST OF SPECIES

The list is in order of appearance in each chapter, with Canadian names shown in brackets.

CHAPTER 1
Canada, March 1983

Polar Bear
Caribou
Wolf

CHAPTER 2
Svalbard, March/April 1984

Polar Bear
Reindeer
Fulmar
Black Guillemot
Ringed Seal
Arctic Fox
Ptarmigan (Rock Ptarmigan)
Common Guillemot (Murre)

CHAPTER 3
Canada, April 1983

Polar Bear
Walrus
Musk Ox
Peary Caribou
Wolf
Beluga Whale
Ringed Seal
Bearded Seal
Raven
Snow Bunting

CHAPTER 4
Canada, May 1984

Amphipods
Ctenophores – comb jellies
Jellyfish
Polar Cod
Caribou
Musk Ox
Ringed Seal
Polar Bear
Clams
Starfish
Sea Squirts
Goby
Squat Lobsters
Copepods
Whales
Guillemot (Murre)
Arctic Char

CHAPTER 5
Canada, May/June 1983

Walrus
Polar Bear
Caribou
Snow Bunting
Wolf
Musk Ox
Lapland Bunting
  (Lapland Longspur)

Greater and Lesser Snow Goose
Sandhill Crane
Whistling Swan
Arctic Fox
Ptarmigan (Rock Ptarmigan)
Grizzly Bear
Canada Goose
Long-tailed Duck (Old Squaw)
Black-throated Diver
  (Arctic Loon)

CHAPTER 6
Greenland, June/July 1984

Sanderling
Snow Bunting
Long-tailed Duck (Old Squaw)
Long-tailed Skua
  (Jaeger)
Barnacle Goose
Varying Lemming
Arctic Hare
Snowy Owl
Arctic Fox
Lapland Bunting
  (Lapland Longspur)
Turnstone (Ruddy Turnstone)
Shore Lark (Horned Lark)
Raven
Black Guillemot
Ptarmigan (Rock Ptarmigan)
Wheatear
Gyrfalcon
Dunlin
Musk Ox
Mosquito
Glaucous Gull
Clouded Yellow Butterfly
Polar Fritillary Butterfly
Crane-fly

CHAPTER 7
Canada, June/July 1983/4

Snowy Owl
Collared Lemming
Brown Lemming
Snow Bunting
Shore Lark (Horned Lark)
Red-throated Diver (Loon)
Long-tailed Duck (Old Squaw)
Long-tailed Skua (Jaeger)
Greater Snow Goose
Grey Phalarope (Red Phalarope)
Turnstone (Ruddy Turnstone)
Grey Plover (Black-bellied
  Plover)
King Eider
Lapland Bunting
  (Lapland Longspur)
Little Stint
Baird's Sandpiper

Arctic Skua (Parasitic Jaeger)
Pomarine Skua
  (Jaeger)
Walrus
Ringed Seal
Ptarmigan (Rock Ptarmigan)
Norway Lemming
Arctic Fox
Mosquito

CHAPTER 8
Canada, July 1984

Barnacle Goose
Brünnich's Guillemot
  (Thick-billed Murre)
Beluga Whale
Narwhal
Walrus
Amphipods
Arctic Cod
Bearded Seal
Harp Seal
Squid
Molluscs
Bowhead Whale
Caribou
Common Eider
Arctic Char
Musk Ox
Wolf
Polar Bear
Ringed Seal
Greater Snow Goose

CHAPTER 9
Canada and Spitsbergen,
July 1983/August 1984

Polar Bear
Ringed Seal
Black Guillemot
Glaucous Gull
Ivory Gull
Brünnich's Guillemot
  (Thick-billed Murre)
Guillemot (Common Murre)
Kittiwake
Fulmar
Little Auk (Dovekie)
Arctic Fox
Barnacle Goose
Arctic Tern

CHAPTER 10
Canada, August 1983

Musk Ox
Peary Caribou
Wolf
Ivory Gull
Turnstone (Ruddy Turnstone)
Sanderling

Polar Bear
Brent Goose (Brant Goose)
King Eider
Long-tailed Duck
Collared Lemming.

CHAPTER 11
Canada, September 1984/
October 1983–4

Caribou
Grizzly Bear
Red Fox
Arctic Fox

Snow Bunting
Shore Lark (Horned Lark)
Arctic Hare
Ground Squirrel
Rough-legged Buzzard
  (Rough-legged Hawk)
Golden Eagle
Wolf
Snowy Owl
Peregrine Falcon
Arctic Skua
  (Parasitic Jaeger)
Whistling Swan

Lake Trout
Arctic Grayling
Raven

CHAPTER 12
Canada, October/November
  1984

Caribou
Polar Bear
Ptarmigan (Willow Grouse)
Ringed Seal

PICTURE CREDITS

12, 13, 17 above & left George Calef; 17 right Birger Amundsen; 28 above left Rasmus Hansson; 28 above right, centre & below left Hugh Miles; 28 below right Mike Salisbury; 29 Hugh Miles; 32 above Birger Amundsen; 32 below, 33 above Hugh Miles; 33 below Mike Salisbury; 36 Thor Larsen; 37 Hugh Miles; 40–41 Ian Stirling; 44 left & right Mike Salisbury; 44 below Rasmus Hansson; 45 left Thor Larsen; 45 right Mike Salisbury; 48 Ian Stirling; 52–53 Bryan & Cherry Alexander; 56, 57 S. D. MacDonald, Canada National Museum of Natural Sciences; 60 above Mike Salisbury; 60 below, 61 above Hugh Miles; 61 below Bryan & Cherry Alexander; 64, 65 left & right Mike Salisbury; 65 below Ian Stirling; 72 Mike Salisbury; 73 Bill Curtsinger/The National Audubon Society Collection/Photo Researchers Inc; 76 above Mike Beedell; 76 below left Ian Stirling; 76 below right, 77 Bryan & Cherry Alexander; 84, 85, 88, 89 George Calef; 92 Mike Read; 96 above Hugh Miles; 96 below Mike Read; 97 above left & right, centre Hugh Miles; 97 below left Mike Read; 97 below right, 100 Hugh Miles; 101 Mike Read; 104 above David Cabot; 104 below, 105, 108 Mike Read; 109 above Anne Gunn; 109 left Lars Knutsen; 109 right David Cabot; 112 Mike Read; 113 above left & right, centre right, below left Hugh Miles; 113 centre left, below right Mike Read; 116, 120 above Brian Hawkes; 120 left & right Mike Salisbury; 121 S. D. MacDonald, Canada National Museum of Natural Sciences; 124–125 Mike Salisbury; 128 above Bryan & Cherry Alexander; 128 left & right George Calef; 129 above, centre & left Mike Salisbury; 129 right Bryan & Cherry Alexander; 132, 133 above Brian Hawkes; 133 below, 136, 140 above Mike Salisbury; 140 below Norman Lightfoot; 141 above Bill Curtsinger/The National Audubon Society Collection/Photo Researchers Inc; 141 below George Calef; 144 Brian Hawkes; 145 Mike Beedell; 148, 149, 152, 153 above & centre Mike Salisbury; 153 below George Calef; 160, 161 Hugh Miles; 164 above Thor Larsen; 164 centre Bryan & Cherry Alexander; 164 left Hugh Miles; 164 right Mike Salisbury; 165 George Calef; 168 Bryan & Cherry Alexander; 169 Hugh Miles; 172 above George Calef; 172 below John Lythgoe/Seaphot; 173 Mike Salisbury; 176 Mike Read; 180, 181, 184, 185 above Mike Salisbury; 185 below Mike Read; 188 above Mike Salisbury; 188 left George Calef; 188 left Lars Knutsen; 189 Mike Read; 192, 196 above George Calef; 196 left Lars Knutsen; 196 right Hugh Miles; 200 above George Calef; 200 below Hugh Miles; 201, 204 George Calef; 205 above Hugh Miles; 205 below Mike Salisbury; 208 George Calef; 213 above Hugh Miles; 213 below Bryan & Cherry Alexander; 217, 221 Bryan & Cherry Alexander.

INUIT ART

pp 9, 21, 81, 117, 137, 222 drawings by Germaine Arnaktauyok from *Stories of Pangnirtung*, published by Hurtig Publishers, Edmonton, Alberta, Canada, and reproduced with permission of the artist; p 177 *Muskox Near Ice* by Pudlo Pudlat, p 209 *Nanu* by Kananginak Pootoogook, both reproduced with the permission of the West Baffin Eskimo Co-operative Limited, Cape Dorset, Northwest Territories, Canada; p 49 *Watchful Walrus* by Solomon Karpik/Imoona Karpik, p 69 *Playful Narwhals* by Malaya Akulukjuk/ Mosesie Nuvaqirq, p 93 *Geese of Summer* by Malaya Teemotee/Imoona Karpik, p 157 *Swimming Bear* by Wayne Neolgana, p 193 *Caribou* by Lypa Pitsiulak, all reproduced with the permission of the Pangnirtung Eskimo Co-operative, Pangnirtung, Northwest Territories, Canada.

223